A NEURODIVERGENT BLOGGER

Yenn Purkis

A NEURODIVERGENT BLOGGER

Posts Highlighting Lived Experience of Self-Determination, Pride, and Empowerment

The Disability Studies Collection

Collection Editors

Damian Mellifont &
Jennifer Smith-Merry

First published in 2024 by Lived Places Publishing
All rights reserved. No part of this publication may be reproduced, stored in a retrieval system, or transmitted in any form or by any means, electronic, mechanical, photocopying, recording or otherwise, without prior permission in writing from the publisher.

No part of this book may be used or reproduced in any manner for the purpose of training artificial intelligence technologies or systems. In accordance with Article 4(3) of the Digital Single Market Directive 2019/790, Lived Places Publishing expressly reserves this work from the text and data mining exception.

The authors and editors have made every effort to ensure the accuracy of information contained in this publication, but assume no responsibility for any errors, inaccuracies, inconsistencies and omissions. Likewise, every effort has been made to contact copyright holders. If any copyright material has been reproduced unwittingly and without permission the Publisher will gladly receive information enabling them to rectify any error or omission in subsequent editions.

Copyright © 2024 Lived Places Publishing

British Library Cataloguing in Publication Data
A CIP record for this book is available from the British Library

ISBN: 9781916985360 (pbk)
ISBN: 9781916985384 (ePDF)
ISBN: 9781916985377 (ePUB)

The right of Yenn Purkis to be identified as the Author of this work has been asserted by them in accordance with the Copyright, Design and Patents Act 1988.

Cover design by Fiachra McCarthy
Book design by Rachel Trolove of Twin Trail Design
Typeset by Newgen Publishing UK

Lived Places Publishing
Long Island
New York 11789

www.livedplacespublishing.com

Abstract

This book consists of an anthology of posts taken from Yenn Purkis' two blog sites, which range in time from 2014 to 2024. Each post is related to a high-level heading and includes reflections on the past and what the author wants to see in the future. The autism and neurodiversity space has changed a lot in the ten years since Yenn started writing for their blog sites. The blog posts are reflective and also illustrate ways forward. The author's intent with the posts is to make changes and open a conversation around neurodiversity and related topics.

The book focuses on a number of areas of relevance to neurodivergent people and allies, including identity and pride, employment, access to services, gender diversity and sexuality, mental health, sensory issues, and more. It is filled with Yenn's personal reflections and wisdom from their 20 years as an autism and Queer advocate and activist. The book is practical and insightful.

The book is full of helpful advice and selections. The lived experience perspective will contribute to knowledge and understanding around autism for a number of groups including neurodivergent individuals, parents of neurodivergent kids, clinicians, teachers, and other support workers. The book illustrates autistic and Queer experiences. It is also an enjoyable and enlightening read for a general audience.

Keywords
- Autism
- Neurodivergent
- Neurodiversity
- Inclusion
- Advocacy
- Non-binary
- Mental health
- Identity
- Empowerment
- Intersectionality

Contents

Content warning   viii
Learning objectives   ix
Introduction   1
Chapter 1   Autistic identity   3
Chapter 2   The social and medical models of disability   29
Chapter 3   Strategies for autistic thriving and being in a good place   43
Chapter 4   Navigating the social world   61
Chapter 5   Gender diversity and sexuality   81
Chapter 6   Managing sensory processing issues   95
Chapter 7   Mental health – places within the mind   107
Chapter 8   Employment and the workplace   121
Chapter 9   Navigating accommodation   131
Epilogue   141
Notes   143
Assignments and discussion points   144
References   145
Recommended further readings   149
Index   151

Content warning

Some of the content in this book may be confronting or upsetting to some readers. Content includes references to:

- Suicide
- Mental health
- Self-harm
- Drug use
- Bullying

Learning objectives

This books aims to help readers in terms of:

1. Exploring the identity and experiences of neurodivergent people;
2. Understanding ways of addressing barriers to inclusion for neurodivergent people;
3. Understanding the author's personal lived experiences;
4. Providing strategies and advice on living well for neurodivergent people; and
5. Promoting understanding of neurodivergent experiences and intersectionality.

Introduction

I am an autistic advocate, author, and presenter. I am also asexual and non-binary, have attention-deficit/hyperactivity disorder (ADHD), have atypical schizophrenia, and have a criminal justice history from the 1990s. Basically, I tick a bunch of intersectional boxes! I have been working in the neurodiversity advocacy space since 2005 when I wrote my first published book – the autobiography *Finding a Different Kind of Normal*. I have been writing ever since and at the time of writing this, I have 17 published books. Advocacy is very dear to my heart, and supporting autistic folks to navigate life well is a bit of a passion for me. As I always say, autistic passions change the world.

I have a big presence in the online world, which is supported through my writing and presentations and my social media engagement. One of the ways that I express myself and promote inclusion, acceptance, and respect in the community is through my blogging. I have two blog sites, the first of which I created in 2014 under my previous name. In 2018, I came out as non-binary, and shortly afterward I changed my name to Yenn. The second blog site is under my affirmed name, Yenn, and has been going since 2019.

I love blogging. It is a way of presenting a specific idea to an audience in an accessible and easy-to-read format. It also challenges me to clarify my thinking on a topic. The blog posts usually take about 20 minutes to draft, 5 minutes to edit, and 5 minutes to post on my various social media platforms. In this sense they are quite immediate. I get in a bit of a zone when I write the blog posts where I am in hyperfocus. I feel quite tired after writing a post as it takes a lot of intense mental energy!

I had the idea for this book when I passed 600 posts on the blog sites. I thought there is a lot of practical advice, personal reflection, and information contained within those 600 posts and that a collated anthology based on the posts might be something people would like to read. This book includes a number of the blog posts across a selection of themes. Content ranges from practical advice to observations to my personal experiences. Each chapter includes a reflection on how things have changed in the 10 years that I have been blogging and also in the 20 years I have been an autistic advocate. This is followed by some blog posts illustrating the topic and then a reflection on where I want things to go in the future to promote inclusion, acceptance, understanding, and respect.

Chapters include autistic identity, employment, the social versus medical models of disability, gender identity and sexuality, mental health, and criminal justice, to name a few.

I hope you enjoy this book. It contains a lot of myself – my passion and love for advocacy and inclusion for autistic folks and my own life experiences.

1
Autistic identity

As human beings, the elements that make up our identity are many and varied. To exist as autistic in the largely neurotypical world can be a big challenge which can be exhausting and draining – but also liberating. Being autistic means we tend to share attributes with other autistic people. Our autism is often a key part of our sense of who we are.

Autism is not a long series of deficits. Many autistic people have some very positive attributes related to their autism (Cooper, 2021). These include:

- Attention to detail;
- Kindness and empathy;
- Connections to nature;
- Pattern thinking;
- Quirky sense of humour;
- Loyalty;
- Creativity; and
- Focus.

There are many elements which can influence autistic identity. In this chapter I have focused on the elements of autistic culture, on the managing of microaggressions, and on the importance of autistic pride and advocacy.

In the first of many informative blog posts to be included in this book, I describe my journey of coming home to autistic identity.

Coming home to autistic identity (Purkis, 2022)

I was one of the first adults in Australia diagnosed with what was then called Asperger's syndrome. It was 1994, I was 20 years old and a prisoner. The diagnostician visited me three times to do the assessment. She said that I satisfied all the *DSM-4* criteria for Asperger's syndrome. I disagreed. There were reasons for this.

My understanding of autism was that it validated all the awful things school bullies had said to me. As my parents had sought the diagnosis – and arranged for the clinician to assess me – I felt that the diagnosis was my parents making excuses for my poor behaviour. I understood it to be a diagnosis of "nerd" and I wasn't a nerd. I was a big scary criminal (well, I thought I was, but hindsight tells me I was masking in order to survive.) Deep down I knew I was autistic, but I really struggled with it.

It was seven years after my diagnosis that I accepted I was autistic. However, I didn't exactly embrace my identity. I was happier telling people I had been in prison than I was saying I was autistic. I very grudgingly accepted my "label" but I didn't like it one bit.

I gradually made peace with my autism diagnosis in 2004 when I met the late author and advocate Polly Samuel. Polly became my friend and mentor. She encouraged me to embrace my identity and also to write my life story. I did both of these things and it was amazing – and the book was published, thrusting me into the world of autism advocacy, whether I wanted it or not!

A couple of years after meeting Polly, I truly accepted and embraced my autistic identity and never looked back. I attended and spoke at a conference in Brisbane. The theme was autistic women and girls (this was long before I embraced my non-binary identity). The first day of the conference was open to everyone, but the second was just for autistic women and girls only. I finally realised that I had come home. My autistic identity became very strong, and I was genuinely proud to be autistic. I still am.

That experience of coming home was amazing and I have not looked back since. While many autistic people receive a diagnosis and immediately embrace their autistic identity, for many others – including me – that acceptance can take longer. It can be hard to process, and many people internalise ableism and this can fuel denial. I know that my experience of coming home to my identity – and autistic "family"– was a liberation and an experience I would wish for any autistic person.

Autistic culture

I am sometimes credited with popularising the concept of autistic culture (Purkis, 2006), a fact that I am actually rather proud of (even though I am one of many who have reached a similar conclusion in this area, and not the first one to do so). In the past, autism was seen as almost entirely negative and something which resulted in parental grief and sadness. The idea of autism as an equally valid way of being to all the other neurotypes is a relatively recent notion. The beauty of autistic culture is that it results in people being viewed as equally worthwhile and their approach and experiences being valid. Rather than being a burden or a tragedy, we are simply people speaking a different "language" and following different customs. I love the concept of autistic culture. Much has been written in the scholarly literature on this topic (e.g. Straus, 2013; Broderick and Ne'eman, 2008). Autistic culture supports positive self-identity for autistic people. The idea of our "neurokin"[1] feeds into this and supports pride and positive self-knowledge (Broderick and Ne'eman, 2018).

Are we speaking the same language? Why autistic communication isn't "wrong" (Purkis, 2018)

Apparently, I get communication "wrong" sometimes when interacting with neurotypical people. They tell me I am coming across in a way which is upsetting for them or confusing or a range of other things. However, when I think about my intentions from the same conversations, I am aware what the other person received was a long way off what I was intending to convey. This always leaves me doubting myself and feeling bad. In fact, it shouldn't. I expressed what I wanted to clearly, but between autistic me and the neurotypical person I was speaking with, the message somehow got lost in translation. I didn't do anything "wrong", and neither did they. It is just that we communicate differently. Autistic communication tends not to be understood as such. Instead, we are viewed as if we were neurotypical people communicating really poorly.

This lack of understanding communication can result in discrimination against autistic people. Neurodiversity is a relatively new concept (Silberman, 2016). When it comes to communication differences, someone doesn't only need to be speaking a different language like French or Japanese, they can also "speak" the language of a different type of neurology. Not everyone communicates in the neurotypical "language". In addition to this, every single one of us sees the world through the lens of our own experience. Autistic people do, neurotypical people do – everyone does. This makes it hard for people to see that someone else might be communicating from a different perspective. I find autistics tend to be better at being aware of this than neurotypical people. This is possibly because being a minority in terms of communication, we have had to "learn" the way of expressing meaning used by our allistic colleagues and peers.

Our different autistic "language" has often been seen as wrong. The basis of Applied Behavior Analysis (ABA) and similar "therapies" for autistic kids lies in this idea that we communicate wrong. Apparently, if we just looked "less autistic" and "fit in better", our lives would be improved. In actual fact, these sorts of "therapies" are often really harmful and do a lot more to make us doubt and dislike ourselves than offer anything very useful in terms of communication (Sequenza, 2018).

Imagine a nation where there is a colonial occupation and the people in that nation are forced to speak the language of the colonial power – English, Spanish, and so on. I liken this to making autistic people change their communication in order to be seen as communicating the same way as the others ("the right way" apparently). I have huge issues with this. I'm happy to (figuratively) learn Spanish, but it needs to be on my terms, not because I'm forced to conform. There is really nothing wrong with my autistic "language".

Some of the key areas where communication and expression differences happen include:

- Honesty. Autistic people tend to be honest by default (Specialisterne, 2022). Lying is difficult or impossible for many of us. In terms of communication style, this means we tend to be very direct and upfront. Many neurotypical people see this as rudeness or as us being needlessly blunt. Conversely, many autistic people dislike the "dishonesty" (e.g. white lies, omissions etc.) we see in our allistic peers, which for them is just usual communication.
- Manipulation and subterfuge. Autistic people often operate only on one level. There is usually no subterfuge or hidden meaning beneath what we say and do. This is often misinterpreted by neurotypical people, who do tend to operate on more than one level so they assume we do too. Not being aware of and respecting this difference can be really confusing and damage relationships.
- Non-verbal cues. Autistic people are often not focused on others' "body language". Many of us don't really know what it is meant to be conveying. Non-autistic people can also misinterpret our own nonverbal signals. This can impact on things like the perception of empathy. I can't really tell if somebody is sad unless they are crying, and even then I may miss it. I have a lot of empathy, and if I know someone is having a hard time, I will be there for them as much as I can. But this can get missed, leading to accusations that I am uncaring.
- Communication and alexithymia. This is also known as emotion blindness. Many autistics experience this and it can make life very difficult, including around perceived meaning. I sometimes don't realise how forthright something

I say seems until afterward, as I wasn't aware I felt passionate, or angry or sad and so on. When challenged on being too forceful on one occasion, I advised I wasn't, and it must have come out wrong. But afterward, when I interrogated my memory of the exchange, I realised I had been quite upset. I just hadn't noticed at the time. Imagine trying to explain that to somebody who didn't understand the differences I was talking about. I think I was seen as being dishonest and making excuses.

It is hard to go through life being misunderstood and judged. It is one of the reasons that I value spending time with my autistic peers – my tribe if you like. I am acutely aware that I am speaking a different language with non-autistic people but often they just don't realise it.

This is a key issue for autistic people navigating the world. There are solutions, and I think a lot of these revolve around increased focus on the value of difference and on basically applying the concept of "different, not less" in interactions between people, autistic, non-autistic, and everyone else!

I would love to support neurotypical people learn to "speak autistic" more. In fact, I think a lot of my work falls into that category.

There are many ways to communicate. Learning the metaphorical language of another person gives you views into their understanding, their culture and their being.

In the future, I want the idea of autistic culture to become more mainstream because it is such an inclusive and helpful lens through which to view neurodiversity and autism more specifically. The idea that we are simply speaking a different language is one which I think lends itself to being supportive of inclusion and respect. I often say to neurotypical people, "if I am an expatriate in your country, then you can be an explorer in mine".

Managing microaggressions

Microaggressions are something that neurodivergent folk – and people from other cohorts facing discrimination – experience all the time. Microaggression is a term used for commonplace verbal, behavioural or environmental slights, whether intentional or unintentional, that communicate hostile or negative attitudes towards people from groups which face disadvantage (*Merriam-Webster's Dictionary, 2023*). When I started out as an advocate, there wasn't a term for this, so it is a relatively new concept. Microaggressions tie in with the concept of unconscious bias. They are not OK – even if they are unintentional, although intentional slights are considerably more problematic than unintentional ones.

Some people turn back the issue on the victim, accusing them of being too sensitive or a "snowflake" and complaining about woke culture. In fact, woke culture is a derogatory way of saying that someone is trying to be respectful and inclusive and understanding of others. I have no idea why a person would elect to be intentionally disrespectful. Microaggressions can have a range of impacts, including low self-confidence, self-loathing, confirming internalised ableism, and social exclusion. This is something which remains an issue and needs to be addressed through changes in societal attitudes and through challenging these sorts of views as they arise. Advocacy by people from marginalised groups can support efforts to challenge this kind of thinking as can support from allies.

A little manifesto – microaggressions, neurodiversity, and gender diversity (Purkis, 2021)

I just returned home after being on a speaker panel for IDAHOBIT (International Day Against Homophobia, Biphobia, Intersex discrimination and Transphobia) at the Australian Capital Territory (ACT) Legislative Assembly. I was firmly wearing my activist hat and was inspired to post about some of the issues and microaggressions I experience as an autistic and transgender person with a mental illness.

I think everyone who belongs to intersectional groups experiences microaggressions. To someone who doesn't belong to any diversity groups, they may seem harmless or minor, but in fact they consolidate disadvantage, invalidation and exclusion and can make people feel very bad about themselves and compound bigotry and discrimination.

This is far from an exhaustive list, and others may experience things that I don't experience. Some of the things which seem to crop up a lot include:

1. Infantilism. I was once asked at a conference, "do you live at home with your mummy"? As I was 40 years old and lived in a property I owned, this one came out of left field. People with disability – and not just intellectual or cognitive differences – experience infantilism like this all the time, and at best it is extremely annoying and at worst it compounds

poor treatment in disability services. I once had a mental health worker who had a facial difference and she was always being treated like a child, as if her character and intellect were governed by what her face looked like. This is just never OK.

2. Language and identity. People have told me, "you shouldn't say you are autistic. You should say you are a 'person with autism.'" This one often comes from disability workers and mental health workers, who presumably attended the same class which covered person-first language. Many autistic people say, "I am autistic" because autism is an integral part of who we are. Also, it isn't OK to tell anyone how they should identify themselves. A person's identity is their own. I guess they say the road to perdition is paved with good intentions, and these people are mostly well intentioned. But it still isn't ever OK to say how someone should identify themselves!

3. Assumptions of incompetence. This one happens all the time and not just for autistic people. They hold the view that I am unable to do whatever thing I am doing due to my autism or my mental illness. This is very invalidating and not OK. I met a senior manager from one of the big four banks at an event at Parliament House once. I thought we were having good conversation until she turned to my non-autistic companion and said, "Oh, but she is very articulate", meaning me. What else would I be but articulate? I write books in my spare time and give TED talks!

4. The very big problem with "normal". I was once told I shouldn't say I am autistic because I could pass for "normal" – whatever that is. The concept of "normal" is highly problematic. It suggests that there is a "norm" of cognitive

or physical functioning and that people deviate from that. It also presupposes that normal is good and deviations from it are not. Normal is a big problem in the disability space particularly. I never use it unless I am discussing shampoo or cycles on the washing machine.

5. "We are all on the spectrum somewhere" – this one is prevalent and not at all OK. The autism spectrum is not a long line with the least autistic person up one end and the most autistic up the other. It doesn't work like that. Also, saying we are all on the spectrum invalidates autistic experience. It is like saying, "oh, but we are all like that so your experience is less significant". This is often said by people who want to connect with us – those good intentions rearing their ugly head again. When people say this to me, I explain why it isn't OK, which usually helps and at least starts a conversation on neurodiversity.

6. Psychiatric misdiagnosis. This happens to a lot of autistic people, especially if the clinician doing the diagnosing doesn't understand a lot about autism. Diagnosis needs to be based on observation and listening, not assumptions. More autism training for mental health workers would be a really good idea. I would volunteer to do it myself!

7. And a couple of microaggressions around gender – or maybe just aggressions, not sure. Misgendering. This is where people use your wrong pronouns, name, or title, and particularly if they do this intentionally or repeatedly. This is not transgender people being picky. Imagine if someone called you "him" if you were a "her"? Imagine if someone called you by the wrong name? And then imagine that you belong to a group which is oppressed and on the receiving

end of hatred, which includes people using the wrong title, name or pronoun. It is not really OK, is it? I and other transgender people experience this repeatedly every single day.

8. The trouble with bathrooms. It can be almost impossible to find a gender-neutral bathroom. Many transgender folks will only use their bathroom at home because of fear of violence should they use a gendered bathroom and because of a lack of gender-neutral bathrooms. I use the gender-neutral bathroom when there is one, and when there isn't, I do a quick conversation with myself as to which gendered bathroom choice is less likely to involve my being attacked if I use it. Some of the time I have more feminine expression than masculine, so on those days I opt for the female-gendered bathroom, but I never feel happy or comfortable going in there.

9. And my final manifesto dot point relates to gender expression. This is broader than my personal experience and it needs to be said. You cannot tell a person's gender just from looking at them. What a person looks like does not, I repeat does not signal their gender identity. People can express their gender in any way they like and that is OK. Actually, it is wonderful.

Challenges with microaggressions, unconscious bias, and unchecked privilege (Purkis, 2023)

I belong to a good number of inclusion / intersectional groups. I am a couple of kinds of neurodivergent, many kinds of Queer, and have a traumatic past which includes some pretty horrific experiences of institutional neglect, incarceration, and associated powerlessness. Every day of my life I am reminded that I am different, that I face disadvantage, that I am seen by some as being "less". I experience everything from unintentional unconscious bias to outright hostility and hatred. It is exhausting.

I will share some of the more memorable microaggressions I have experienced since coming out as non-binary. I came out in 2018 for the first time on Facebook (as you do!!). A trans friend told me I would discover who my friends were, who they weren't, and that it would surprise me. They were absolutely correct. Some people reacted the way I expected but not everyone did. Social media can be a scary place, and it is full of bigots but also people who might be well meaning but who come out with some doozies in terms of bias and microaggression. My favourite was the person who said I couldn't wear a skirt if I was non-binary because skirts were for girls. I wondered if this meant I shouldn't wear pants either given that they are gendered male. Who knew?? Another one was the person who insisted that my Facebook page was about autism not gender, and I should stop talking about gender on my page. I mean, it is my page. I could post about bunnies if I so desired or Lego or the music of Bjork!

It is not confined to the world of gender diversity. As an autistic person, I have been on the receiving end too. Countless people have said to me, "we are all on the spectrum somewhere", and many others have told me off for identifying as "autistic"! Some of these comments probably come from ignorance and unchecked privilege, but the gender-based ones tend to be the most likely place for outright hatred and the autism ones tend to be due to ableism and ignorance.

I have been trolled by strangers and "friends" alike. Someone even managed to say something horrible about my late and very much missed moggie Mr. Kitty. What kind of hatred does a person have to have to attack a dead cat?

Last weekend I had a workshop which was in a building in Barton. Apart from the organisation running the workshop, there was one staff member from the building. At morning tea, this person was quite patronising to me – I must have been wearing my "Disabled" sticker! Then shortly after that, I needed the toilet, but I didn't know where it was. The staff member from the building said to me without hesitating, "the ladies is that way". I am fairly certain she was trying to be helpful, but it really upset me. I wish people would not assume gender – and particularly MY gender! I was talking about it to a friend today and she said that most people would assume gender when they saw me, and I understand that but it just upsets me. I rarely assume gender based on looking at a person – although I admit I have done it before. For me, a person could be any gender and wear any kind of clothes. I am not going to assume they are a particular gender. Surely this is why we introduce ourselves with our pronouns.

It is a full-time job managing all the bigoted nonsense that is out there. We need a lot more understanding of trans experience and we need more positive representation of trans and gender-divergent folks. Once again, things are improving, particularly in the neurodiversity space, but there is still a long way to go.

I educate people where I can. Some activists say we shouldn't have to educate ignorant people, but I am always happy to educate – although I agree that other people's bigotry and bias is not my responsibility to fix!

I am lucky in this area. I am a confident, accomplished autistic, non-binary, and asexual person. I don't take crap! I am an alpha personality too, and am more than happy to pull someone up if they do the wrong thing – gently leading those who don't mean it and challenging those where there is intent. Sometimes people say, "I can't use your pronouns because it is too hard". That is a common remark I have got over the years, and I have to turn it around and explain how it feels for me to be misgendered.

I think things are improving in this space but there is never room for complacency. There are plenty of people who would have me simply because I am non-binary. So keep flying the flag for inclusion in all its forms, and if in doubt, ask a trans person.

I think the key to addressing microaggressions involves a number of things. Firstly, understanding of difference is essential. People need to check their bias and privilege and if need be, undertake training in addressing bias or just reading content by those from intersectional groups. Also, understanding the impact of microaggressions is really important. This involves a good whack of empathy. And we need better representation of autistic folks – and those from other intersectional groups – in every aspect of life: media, politics, business and entrepreneurship, popular culture, social media – everywhere! People also need to be able to recognise when they are delivering a microaggression and stop themselves from doing it. This shouldn't be too hard. I have white privilege, but I manage not to utter racial slurs, and if I slip up due to my privilege, I will apologise and resolve to not repeat the problem communication. I think a world where people had a greater awareness of autistic experience and saw us through the lens of autistic pride, autistic culture, and the neurodiversity paradigm would be a better world for all of us.

Autistic pride and advocacy

Being proud in your identity is a wonderful thing. Autistic pride makes a big difference for autistic people and is a huge positive. Autistic people have the right to be proud of who we are and to see our identity as a positive. Autistic pride is about liking and valuing yourself just as you are. It makes life so much better for autistic folks. However, autistic pride is a relatively new concept.

I was diagnosed as autistic in 1994. At that time, pretty much all the dialogue about autism was negative and deficits-based. Autistic kids were seen as a burden and autism as a tragedy. Being autistic was definitely not viewed as a reason for pride; rather, it was a reason for grief and sadness. When I started advocating for inclusion for neurodivergent folks in 2005, the narrative around autism was still mostly negative. Even for me, my autism was still something I wasn't very happy about.

Something happened to change my view and that was meeting autistic author and my first autistic mentor, Polly Samuel. I learned my own sense of pride in Polly's house, which was full of art, books, and stimmy things. Shortly after meeting Polly, I wrote my first book, an autobiography. But for many other autistic people at the time and those who loved and cared for them, pride was still a long way off.

One thing that demonstrates the growth of autistic pride is the days which we celebrate. When I started advocating, the day for autism awareness was 2 April. Organisations which were certainly not promoting autistic pride but were flying the flag for deficits thinking and ableism, encouraged people to light it up blue for autism. Many autistic people – including me – found this offensive and disrespectful because the organisations promoting it were primarily quite ableist, and we felt they did not have the welfare of autistic people in mind. Then we had a number of autistic-led organisations promoting lighting it up different colours to reflect inclusion and respect. At the time, most mainstream autism organisations were supporting Autism "awareness" day on 2 April and lighting things up blue. Not long after this, there was something of a seismic shift. Mainstream organisations started celebrating Neurodiversity Pride Day on 18 June. They started agreeing with the complaints from autistic people that awareness alone wasn't enough and we need other things to support autistic folks, such as respect, understanding, acceptance, and inclusion. Now the whole argument around lighting things up blue and marking awareness is almost a thing of the past, but even so, there are still a lot of autistic people who do not feel a sense of pride.

Autistic pride and self-advocacy is a relatively recent phenomenon (Silberman, 2016). When I started my own advocacy journey in 2005, there were hardly any other visible autistic advocates and we were very much marginalised. The attitudes at the time were primarily that autism was entirely negative; it was viewed as a curse and a tragedy and autistic people were seen as having very little – or nothing – to offer the world. Autistic pride was not a common attitude. In wider society, autism was hardly known and the information most people could access related to not very accurate portrayals of a few autistic characters in popular culture such as the film *Rain Man*. People who promoted autistic pride and positive identity were few and far between, and autistic people were not expected to have anything to add to the conversation. Being proud of who you are is an excellent thing for people from any group. For autistic folks, advocacy and self-advocacy can result in a greater degree of positive self-knowledge and pride. To advocate for yourself often comes from a position of thinking you are a valued and worthwhile person who deserves respect and understanding, not bigotry, bullying, or disrespect. Self-advocacy can support positive identity for autistic folks.

A parent's guide to autistic pride, (Purkis, 2018)

A good friend who is a non-autistic parent of autistic kids asked autistic people to write out some thoughts for parents in relation to Autistic Pride Day on 18 June. I thought this was a good thing to do. My responses to her questions have been adapted into this post. As an autistic advocate with over 13 years' experience, I have seen a lot of changes in the autism world. When I started out in 2005, many parents were very heavily focused on the negatives around autism and would express – often in front of their kids – what a burden it was to have an autistic child. Thankfully this has become a much rarer occurrence, but there are still some misunderstandings which can occur between autistic advocates and non-autistic parents. I think connecting with parents – and particularly non-autistic ones – is really important. The biggest influence on a child's life is more often than not their parent/s. Autistic pride is a really important topic for all families with one or more autistic members and probably more broadly in society, so I thought I would write this post. I hope you find it helpful.

Autistic pride is premised on the notion that autistic people are valuable, worthy, and an important part of human society just as they are, as autistic people. This does not mean they will not experience difficulties with some areas of life, or that they don't need support. But it does mean recognising and fostering their strengths, talents, and interests and supporting them to like and value themselves.

Despite there being a lot more awareness and understanding of autism in recent years, we are still discriminated against. This is demonstrated in a number of settings from the still appallingly high rates of bullying of autistic kids in schools to the very low employment participation rates and low educational attainment statistics.

Autistic pride is a great way to counter this. If a person is genuinely proud of who they are and sees their autism in a positive light, as part of their character and personality, it helps them navigate the world better. This is relevant for all autistic people – those who use verbal speech and those that don't, those with all cognitive abilities and accomplishments and those with any additional "labels" as well as autism. It is a quality that parents can play a huge part in fostering and supporting.

Pride feeds into a bunch of very useful attributes like self-esteem, self-confidence, resilience, and independence. Even better, it allows us to value ourselves in the face of a world that often does not respect or value us, and to educate others and advocate for other autistic people too. Someone who is filled with a sense of pride and self-respect is more likely to navigate life well, be fulfilled in life and achieve their potential. Without that sense of pride, and given all the barriers stacked against us, it can be very hard to be who we want and need to be. Pride is great at helping level the playing field for autistic people. It is one of those qualities which is pretty much always a good thing. The example that a person who is proud of who they are sets for others is fantastic, and it also demonstrates a model of viewing autism through the lens of pride. This will almost certainly impact on neurotypical people and change their understanding of autism for the better.

There are many sorts of messages and actions non-autistic parents and other adults can do to promote and foster a sense of pride in autistic kids and young people. These include:

- Understanding that autism is a different wiring of the brain and not due to a deficient or "broken" brain;
- Understanding that autistic communication is as valuable and effective as non-autistic communication – just put a roomful of autistic people together and take notice of how they don't have the kind of miscommunications as they might when communicating with non-autistic people;
- Viewing communication this way and having a sense of needing to learn to "speak autistic" is a key part of understanding autistic young people and fostering a sense of pride;
- Reading and viewing work by other autistic people – there are advocates who are children as well as adults and they often have some very useful strategies and understanding too;

- Making sure your child has access to autistic people as possible friends, and also adult role models and mentors where appropriate. Adult autistics can be great translators and interpreters for kids, and kids interacting with autistic adult role models is a very powerful way to build their self-esteem and sense of pride;
- Not punishing a child for "autistic" activities like stimming. And not fixating on or insisting on eye contact, or on things perceived as "poor social skills" that are just a bit different (e.g. parallel play at later ages than that at which neurotypical kids might stop doing it); and
- Encouraging kids. Taking an interest in their interests. Challenging and stretching them within their capacity so they will be proud of themselves for overcoming challenges.

Thoughts on some "therapies" to avoid

Parents of autistic kids, especially newly diagnosed kids, want answers and want to help their child in whatever way they can. This is of course completely understandable, but it is important to be aware there are lots of charlatans peddling pseudoscience "cures" and "treatments". Often these individuals view autism as an "epidemic" or something that a person can recover from. If any individual or company talks about "cures" and "recovery", it is a good idea to avoid these at all cost. They won't help your child and they will probably do more harm than good.

At the same time, beware of "evidence-based" therapies that are centred around compliance.

It is very rare indeed for a parent to intentionally do something harmful to their child. Unfortunately, some "therapies" which are marketed as being helpful and enabling your child to get along better in the non-autistic world, are in fact focused on conditioning your child to act "less autistic". This alone can have a huge negative impact on how your child views themselves.

This sort of "therapy" does not support autistic children to develop into happy, fulfilled autistic adults. Instead, it works to forcibly make a child seem less autistic. We don't need to make autistic children try to look less autistic! We need to support them to be themselves, and if anyone has an issue with their stimming – or whatever – well, that person needs to be educated. There are a lot of documented cases of trauma in autistic adults who went through these "therapies", which are essentially conversion therapy, as kids. I am certain their parents did not intentionally subject them to this knowing it would cause trauma. It would most likely have been promoted to those parents as a therapy to make their child somehow "better". Sadly, this kind of thing rewards kids for doing often very stressful and unpleasant things like making eye contact. It can also remove some of the child's effective coping mechanisms. For example, stimming is used by many autistic kids as a means to self-regulate and address stress. You can imagine the impact that removing that one strategy might have on a child (Kupferstein, 2018).

These kinds of "therapies" do not help kids develop pride and value in themselves. In fact, they could be seen as representing the enemy or as the antithesis of autistic pride.

I speak with parents every day and have given countless presentations to parent groups. But I am not a parent myself, and my perspective in this piece is that of an autistic adult who has only relatively recently developed a sense of pride in who I am as an autistic person. If I had had that sense of self-worth and pride as a kid going through all the horrors I did, I know it would have made a huge difference. Pride is a gift you can support your child to attain.

Thank you.

Neurodiversity Pride Day – Reflections on what Pride actually means (Purkis, 2022)

Today is Neurodiversity Pride Day. Big yay to that! But I must admit that pride doesn't really sum up how I feel today. Let me explain… Yesterday, I discovered that a hacker had stolen $8,600 from my credit card. Anyone would struggle with that, but for me it was especially traumatic. I have been very anxious about online security for the past year. By anxious I mean the kind of anxiety that results in psychosis and suicide attempts (I speak from unfortunate experience on both of those things). When I realised yesterday that I had been hacked, I was in a world of stress. I am going to need to contact the bank later today to find out what the person at the bank that I spoke to yesterday actually said, because I was so stressed, I missed most of it!

So I am not feeling at all proud – mostly feeling very stressed and depressed and uncertain about anything I used to take for granted in terms of security. But it is Neurodiversity Pride Day and

I am not only multiply neurodivergent but I am also an advocate. So, I am proud within all of that fear and misery.

So, what does Neurodiversity Pride Day even mean? Why should I be proud? What does pride do for me as a neurodivergent person who is managing a lot of stress at present?

Well, to my mind pride is all about owning your identity and celebrating achievements – and often celebrating our survival in a world that doesn't always value or support us. I should feel proud to be a neurodivergent survivor, someone who has struggled in life due to ableism and the medical model of disability and discrimination and bullying based on my neurotype. I should celebrate my neurodivergent culture. I should celebrate the fact that there are now so many advocates out there with their message of encouragement, empowerment, and activism.

I started doing this in 2005 (cue groan from audience who have heard the "Yennski has been an advocate for almost twenty years" statement many times before…). Anyway, when I started, there were just a few advocates active in the neurodiversity space, most of them being autistic people. There were a handful of books written by autistic authors – including my first book. There was a neurodiversity movement but it was in its early stages. I remember that parents of autistic kids often had some really unhelpful views. Advocacy was very hard and people talking about the strengths of autistic people was rare. People now call me – and presumably my colleagues who were working alongside me in the early 2000s and those active in the 1990s – a trailblazer in the advocacy community. Flash forward to now, and the neurodiversity approach is frequently taken on board by people who in the past would have been giving me a hard time and telling me that "you don't speak on behalf of my child" or "my child is severely autistic and you are mild" and so on.

On Pride Day, I want to celebrate all my fellow advocates – whether they have been active for 20 years or 2 months, whether they are 70 or 17. There are so many of us now with all our different perspectives, and it is a good thing.

Pride is not just about celebrating achievements though. It is about acknowledging the work and contribution of neurodivergent people and the challenges that we have faced and overcome. Pride is about identity – about owning who you are. Pride is about knowing that you have limitations and that life can be challenging but engaging with it anyway. You don't have to be happy to be proud, and often for neurodivergent folks, happiness can be a difficult thing to attain.

I am proud to be autistic and an ADHDer. I am even proud to have a schizophrenia diagnosis – although I'm not sure if there is a pride day for that (maybe I should create one…). Pride is such an important thing for members of groups that face disadvantage in society. So today I am sad and stressed but also very proud. I have survived in a world which hasn't always been very supportive or inclusive and I am still here, still advocating, still fighting for a better world.

I recognise my fellow neurodivergent people on this day. I see so many people advocating for a better world for neurodivergent folks. We have gone from a handful of people to a huge movement which has rewritten the script about neurodiversity and inclusion. Big yay to that. And happy Pride Day!

Conclusion

In the future, I want autistic people liking and valuing ourselves to be the norm. I want us not to feel we have to hide who we are and mask and pretend to be something we are not. I want neurotypical and allistic people to have a greater understanding of why we need pride and to recognise our strengths and unique qualities. I want pride to be the norm, and I want autistic folks to be able to be confident in ourselves.

I think we are well placed to support all neurodivergent people to be proud of who they are. By "we" I mean autistic advocates, our allies, and organisations working for positive change as well as neurodivergent individuals with no particular claims on advocacy but who are just trying to live their life well. We need to build on the gains already made and avoid complacency. I want autistic folks all to have a profound sense of pride, and with it, self-acceptance, self-confidence, and self-respect. Given the changes in the past 20 years, I think this is a highly attainable goal.

The blog posts from the past few years that have been included in this chapter demonstrate a need for respect and understanding for autistic folks. They show how we can be proud of who we are and the need to address microaggressions and bias . Identity is a huge issue for people from any intersectional / inclusion groups. We need a sense of pride and to address self-doubt and to work with our peers to change the world. While things have improved in many areas, it is essential not to be complacent and to ensure we continue to challenge negative attitudes, bigotry, and hatred.

2
The social and medical models of disability

For those of us working in the disability and inclusion space, the concept of the social versus the medical model is probably one we have run into in our travels. People with Disability Australia describes the social and medical models of disability on its website (People with Disability Australia, 2022):

> "According to the medical model, "disability" is a health condition dealt with by medical professionals. People with disability are thought to be different to "what is normal" or abnormal. "Disability" is seen "to be a problem of the individual.
>
> From the medical model, a person with disability is in need of being fixed or cured. From this point of view, disability is a tragedy and people with disability are to be pitied. The medical model of disability is all about what a person cannot do and cannot be.
>
> The social model sees "disability" is the result of the interaction between people living with impairments and an

environment filled with physical, attitudinal, communication and social barriers. It therefore carries the implication that the physical, attitudinal, communication and social environment must change to enable people living with impairments to participate in society on an equal basis with others.

A social model perspective does not deny the reality of impairment nor its impact on the individual. However, it does challenge the physical, attitudinal, communication and social environment to accommodate impairment as an expected incident of human diversity."

These models are particularly relevant for autistic people. When I started my advocacy journey in 2005, I observed that the medical model was quite prevalent. Parents of autistic kids would be told by medical specialists everything that was apparently wrong with their child and how they should try to make them somehow "less autistic". As an autistic person, I found this highly problematic, but the view appeared to be everywhere.

More recently, I have observed a change in this space, and not just from autistic advocates and activists. Allistic authors like Steve Silberman (*Neurotribes*) and Graeme Simison (author of the "*Rosie*" trilogy – Simsion, 2015) worked with autistic people and presented sympathetic views of neurodivergent experience, be that in fiction or non-fiction. The terms "neurodiversity" and "neurodivergence" are now in common parlance, when in the past they were mostly used by neurodivergent people only. These terms are often used incorrectly, and with neurodiverse used instead of neurodivergent. Everyone is neurodiverse – it means having a diverse neurology, which we all have. Neurodivergent means having a neurology that diverges from neurotypical such as autistic, ADHD, dyslexia, anxiety, and so on.

The medical model to my mind is less helpful than the social one and can deny autistic people the opportunity to shine. The medical model also puts the "blame" for any issues on the apparently problematic autistic person, which is neither helpful nor accurate! Neurodivergent people have the right to make informed choices about their medical treatments such as the decision to take medication.

Note: The next blog post is (I think) my most viewed and commented on post of all time. It had over 5,000 views on the blog site. While it is intended to be humorous, it also has a strong message about the benefit of viewing autism through the lens of the social model of disability.

Blog posts on the social and medical models of disability

The *DSM-5* autism criteria rewritten with neurodiversity in mind (Purkis, 2015)

While working on a book about mental illness, I had to dig out the diagnostic criteria for Autism in the *DSM-5* (American Psychiatric Publishing, 2013) It made me sad, so I decided to whip out my advocate brush and give it a neurodiversity-based touch-up. I hope you like it. I'm not sure how a doctor would use it, but I prefer it to the original version. The way it works is that I have listed each category of the *DSM-5* diagnostic criteria for Autism in italics and underneath have redrafted it. Enjoy.

A. Persistent deficits in social communication and interaction across multiple contexts, as manifested by all of the following (currently or by history):

1. Deficits in social-emotional reciprocity
2. Deficits in non-verbal communication behaviours used for social interaction
3. Deficits in developing, maintaining, and understanding relationships

Specify current severity based on social communication impairments and restricted, repetitive patterns of behaviour.

A ("Ausome" (a term meaning awesome and autistic). Different ways of communicating and relating to others. This is part of the person's basic make-up. It is not a deficit or a disability; it is just a different way of communicating. Some ways in which this might be demonstrated include:

1. Different ways of relating and experiencing emotions. Some people may have hyperempathy. They may make excellent psychologists or counsellors.
2. Interacting in different ways. Being honest and straightforward and not generally using things like manipulation or sarcasm.
3. Approaching relationships differently to non-autistic people. People may be very loyal and/or have strong bonds with an individual or small group of friends. Autistic people often have a great connection with non-human "people" too and a connection to the natural world.

B. Restrictive, repetitive patterns of behaviour, interests or activities, as manifested by at least two of the following, currently or by history:

1. Stereotyped or repetitive motor movements, use of objects, or speech
2. Insistence on sameness, inflexible adherence to routines, or ritualised patterns of verbal or non-verbal behaviour
3. Highly restricted, fixated interests that are abnormal in intensity or focus
4. Hyper- or hypo-activity to sensory input or unusual interest in sensory aspects of the environment

B (Beautiful). May be experts in a particular area, have a strong focus and determination. May have very strong interests in a topic, and activities related to these interests may result in a great sense of joy and satisfaction.

Innovative and imaginative use of objects.

Creativity. The ability to follow a schedule. Seeing patterns in things – very useful if the person wants to work for the police as an investigator or be a mathematician or climate scientist. Passionate engagement in a particular interest. As life progresses, autists can develop a huge general knowledge based on all the topics they may have been interested in. Very useful if the person wants to be a university professor. Also, the interests can form an excellent self-soothing tool should the person be depressed.

Exceptional, accurate, and perceptive sensory skills. This is highly useful in areas like catering and viticulture.

C. Symptoms must be present in the early developmental period (but may not become fully manifest until social demands exceed limited capacities, or may be masked by learned strategies in later life).

C (Curious and Clever)

Young children may be quirky, smart, and individualistic. As they grow older, the world can dampen their amazing spirit, but they should not be disheartened as autistic people are often resilient and resourceful.

D. Symptoms cause clinically significant impairment in social, occupational, or other important areas of current functioning.

D (Diverse) The weight of a world which often does not value or respect autistic people can mean that they struggle to navigate life. This is not due to their inherent deficiencies; rather, it is mostly a result of a focus on some arbitrary "norm". With the right support, understanding, and self-confidence, autistic people can rise above this and be their best "them". This is an area for further work.

E. These disturbances are not better explained by intellectual disability (intellectual developmental disorder) or global developmental delay.

E (Exceptional). Autistic people are autistic people. They are amazing as is and defy this sort of diagnostic negativity through their brilliance.

Individuals with a well-established diagnosis of autistic disorder, Asperger's disorder, or pervasive developmental disorder not otherwise specified should be given the diagnosis of autism spectrum disorder. Individuals who have marked deficits is social communication, but whose symptoms do not otherwise meet criteria for autism spectrum disorder, should be evaluated for social (pragmatic) communication disorder.

Autistic folks should be given a diagnosis of "human being" along with all other human beings. We are all pretty much the same and just a little bit different from each other.

The medical model and the social model of disability and the future of diagnosis (Purkis, 2023)

I was in a meeting of neurodivergent folks last week which involved a panel presentation. One of the presenters spoke about their concerns with the medical model of neurodivergent conditions and why they had not sought a diagnosis but instead self-identified. This got me thinking about all of those issues around the medical model.

Basically, there is a medical model of disability and a social model. Under the medical model, we are seen as being disabled by our health condition. Autism, for example, is seen as a disorder or a set of deficits to be somehow fixed. There are some ads on YouTube at the moment featuring an autism researcher proudly saying that we can now give very young autistic kids interventions which mean they will no longer have as many autistic characteristics. More about that later…

The social model of disability is the one I prefer. The social model sees society as the main reason for disability. We become disabled by the world we live in – complete with its assumptions, judgements, and stereotypes. Under the medical model, I am disabled by my neurotype/s. I apparently need some interventions to fix my autistic bits and my schizophrenic bits as they are a deviation from some norm of existence and as such need to be addressed. Under the social model, the world needs to change to support my needs. I do not need fixing, but I need understanding, respect, and support.

The idea of a diagnosis of neurodivergent conditions is in and of itself quite problematic. Within the neurodiversity movement there are conversations around the difficulties with medical diagnosis. If we are not broken and do not need to be fixed, the concept of a medical diagnosis is problematic. Will we have diagnoses in the future, or will our identity as neurodivergent be seen as a valid difference – much like being LGBTQIA+? I mean we don't need a diagnosis of gay – it is a way people are and they know that they are. It is part of their identity. So similarly, in the future will neurodivergence be an identity in a similar way? I am not sure, but it is an interesting thought.

I am seeing more and more people identifying as neurodivergent and embracing their identity. It is a lovely thing. So how do we reconcile the medical model which, at the moment at least, is the dominant paradigm, with the social model and the empowerment which comes along with it? Will there be a need for a medical diagnosis in the future? Will autism and other neurodivergent experiences simply be seen as another way of being?

I see these issues as being critical at the moment. There is disagreement between advocates of the medical model and of the social model (cue autism researcher from the start of this piece proudly saying how his organisation can make kids less autistic). Disagreements around effective supports and therapies are getting more and more fraught and heated.

I want a world where autistic people are accepted and supported to be ourselves. I do not see a world where all the autistic kids have been "fixed" as a good thing. I strongly believe that autistic and other neurodivergent folks offer the world amazing things. We have the right to exist as we are, and we are perfectly valid the way we are. I don't want to be fixed. My autism is a big part of what makes me who I am and I am Yenn Purkis – as far as I can tell, a lot of other people like me just the way I am as well.

A problematic dichotomy: Autistic pride and accessing disability funding (Purkis, 2020)

I recently published a meme about why I remove the "D" in "ASD" as I don't see autism as a disorder but a different way of being. The meme generated a lot of interest and responses, mostly in agreement with my statement. However, someone commented that if we didn't have the deficits / medical approach, autistic people would be unable to access services and funding.

This is a conundrum I have considered for many years and I want to unpack it here. I will start by saying that this is one of those areas of nuance / greyness, and I don't really have a solution to it. The medical / deficits model views autism and other neurodivergences as a disorder and a negative thing. In order to access funding, people need to provide their level of disability and convince funding bodies – such as the National Disability

Insurance Scheme (NDIS) in Australia – that they need help. However, the social / strengths-based / neurodiversity models state that autism and other neurodivergences form a different but equally valid way of being. If you are a proud autistic who needs funding, this presents a challenge!

I use the neurodiversity / strengths-based models as the basis of my work, but this does not mean I think autistics do not need services and funding. However, if I went into a meeting intended to determine funding, I would place the emphasis on my needs and challenges. As a very honest autistic, I struggle with this as I feel like I am letting down the neurodiversity movement by placing a focus on my challenges related to my autism, but at the same time I need to access services to enable me to navigate the world.

The term "neurodiversity" was coined in the 1990s in a bid to fight stigma against neurodivergent people, particularly around autism, ADHD, and dyslexia (Silberman, 2016). Organisations like the Autistic Self Advocacy Network and individuals like Polly Samuel and Wenn Lawson worked to create a more inclusive world for neurodivergent people. Since then, the movement has grown significantly and supports people who are neurodivergent to focus on developing their strengths and talents and be included and respected. The movement is premised on the concepts of "different not less" and "nothing about us without us" (Autistic Self Advocacy Network, 2024).

The problem seems to be the difference in intent and objectives for the two different approaches. If I want to feel good about myself and feel positive about neurodiversity and difference,

I need to put my "autistic pride" hat on. The intent I have is based in neurodiversity pride. Conversely, if I need to access funding, my intent is funding, so I will do what I need to access this – I will put my "medical model" hat on. This is not to say one or the other is right or wrong – just that the objective determines the approach. The two approaches are almost impossible to reconcile to each other.

I am the co-author of a book with Tanya Masterman for autistic kids (Masterman and Purkis, 2020). The book is called the *Awesome Autistic Go-To Guide*. You may have come across it in your travels. I think this book strikes a good balance between the models. The book is premised on autistic pride and positive self-knowledge. But that being said, it also includes advice for kids about managing the challenges autistic kids can face. I recognise that there are difficulties which autistic children can face. These difficulties include being socially isolated, facing bullying, not having sensory issues be addressed, experiencing communication issues, being subjected to therapies which are harmful, and facing discrimination around other intersectional groups these children may belong to (such as transphobia, racism or sexism) (Aspect / Autism Spectrum Australia, 2022).

While I am a strong proponent of the strengths-based model and autistic pride, this does not mean that I think autism is free from challenges. Being autistic can pose a lot of difficulties, from overload and meltdowns to sensory issues and hyperempathy . I saw the term "blissfully autistic" used once, which I took to mean having such a strengths focus as to think autism was a superior state of being.

There is a concept called "supercrip", which can be defined as a stereotyped narrative showing the experience of someone who has "to fight against his/her impairment" and as such is promoted as having superpowers (Martin, 2017). This ties in with the idea of "inspiration porn" coined by the late Stella Young in her excellent TED talk entitled "I'm not your inspiration, thank you very much". The concept of Disabled people as being "inspirational" or having superpowers is highly unhelpful. Autistic folks can be subject to this attitude and it does more harm than good.

I think being autistic is an equally valid and reasonable state to being allistic. We are different, they are different, and that is OK.

It is important to note that every autistic person is different, and things which one person may struggle with may not be a problem for others. There is a saying that if you have met one autistic person, you have met one autistic person.

I think it may be possible to reconcile the strengths-based model and the need for the medical / supports base. I would love to see a way of doing this which enabled autistic people to feel proud of who we are and to see our very real strengths and positives, while being able to access the supports, including medical supports and accommodations that we might need. But as it stands now, this dichotomy is something I struggle with. I want to keep the Disorder out of AS, as I think it is damaging to our sense of who we are. I think too much emphasis is currently placed on the deficits and medical model. Of course, we need supports and services, but we also need to recognise – and be recognised for – the great positives that we bring to the world.

Conclusion

As I stated before, I think the social model is more helpful than the medical one – not just for autistic people but for the wider world. It provides a more positive view and gives autistic people the opportunity to shine free from negative messaging around our needing fixing .

This is not to say that autism doesn't come with some challenges but to also recognise that society has a significant impact – complete with all its expectations, biases, ableism, and barriers that autistic people come up against through no fault of our own. Autism often involves challenges yet so does allistic or neurotypical experience, but we don't pathologise that and see it as a deviation from some unrealistic norm!

I have seen some positive change over the past few years. This is evidenced through the advocacy of people like Chloe Hayden (Chloe Hayden, 2023) and Summer Farrelly. Autistic perspectives have become a lot more common in popular culture and in society more broadly . There are some areas which are challenging, especially around accessing services. I think there needs to be a demedicalisation of our challenges. For example, if someone has a sensory issue, the intervention should be to address that, but without any messaging around it being a pathology. Neurotypical and non-Disabled folks often have challenges, but they generally aren't viewed through the lens of being different from the norm. Supports should be about just that – support – doing what someone needs in order to engage with life. We need to address these issues without the deficits thinking .

Also, the whole "autism is my superpower" concept is something I struggle with. It is just as othering to my mind as the deficits thinking. I do some things really well. I can write pretty much anything, I am an accomplished artist, and I can hop up on stage and give a talk with no worries whatsoever! You might say these are my superpowers. However, there are things I can't do which others can. I can't drive, and I would be a horrible parent. But would I say to a neurotypical person when they are giving me a lift, "Wow! Your driving is amazing. You didn't even have an accident. It is your superpower!" Yes, that is fairly patronising and unhelpful.

What I really want to see is the medical model being more the marginalised view, and I want people to ditch deficits thinking, the pathologising of autistic experience, and the superpower nonsense. And maybe I need to talk to the American Psychological Association about adding my revised autism criteria to the next edition of the *DSM*!

3
Strategies for autistic thriving and being in a good place

Self-advocacy

Advocacy is a major part of what I do. My advocacy tends to be about putting things into the world that promote inclusion and respect for autistic folks and Queer folks. When I started out, I didn't know what I was actually doing! I had a book about my life as an autistic young person, aptly subtitled "Misadventures with Asperger Syndrome" (Purkis, 2006) – and there were a great many misadventures! Autism advocacy wasn't really a "thing" until quite recently where it has grown in magnitude and influence. I want to see a world where autistic people feel comfortable and empowered to advocate for themselves.

Some reasons why we really need autism advocacy (Purkis, 2016)

I watched a movie for my movie night on Friday called *Please Stand By*. It is about an autistic young woman living in California. I won't give spoilers in case you watch it, but it got me thinking about why advocacy is so necessary. Attitudes towards the autistic protagonist were very much that she had no capability to live independently and little to add to the world, but as the film unfolds, it becomes clear that the young woman is highly talented and resourceful. I'm not sure of the disability politics of the filmmaker but I enjoyed the film – except the disturbing bits about Applied Behaviour Analysis,[2] which were very hard to watch. When the film ended, I said to my movie night visitors "I need to write a blog post about this". In fact, my blog post is a bit broader than the film. I am not a movie reviewer! The thing which struck me most about the film is that it demonstrated quite well why advocacy is so important.

The film showed this through:

- Highlighting that many people view autistic people as incompetent and like perennial children.
- Suggesting there are "therapies" for autistic kids which essentially mirror training a dog. This needs to stop.
- Suggesting autistic people often have so much to offer the world, but this is not noticed or understood by many people.

I believe that there is still a view held by some that autistic people have no feelings or empathy. This also has to stop.

In terms of the "real" world, I have been knowingly advocating since 2005. Things have certainly changed since then, but there are still things which really need attention. I – and presumably other autistic speakers – used to only be viewed as a token or the "colour and light" when I gave a talk at autism events, but now there is a growing knowledge that autistic people are the experts in autistic experience (I know, hey, who would have thought??!). There are autistic-led organisations like Yellow Ladybugs and the I CAN Network doing great work in empowering autistic young people. Autistic viewpoints are often featured in news media and not only as "human interest". I see these developments as good things.

However, there are many areas where the situation around inclusion requires significant work. These areas include:

Employment. We are mournfully underrepresented in employment numbers, and in Australia we are almost six times more likely to be unemployed than the general population (Amaze, 2023). This lack of employment is not usually because we are unskilled or unemployable but rather due to a range of factors – some structural and others related to the attitudes of individual employers and to there being a load of unwritten rules at work that we do not understand or notice. This means our skills and talents may be overlooked and employment can be difficult or impossible when, in fact, this does not need to be the case.

Education. We have far lower education attainment levels than the general population (Amaze, 2023). Our children often leave school due to bullying or other issues and simply never go back. Higher education can also be a fraught place for autistics. While schools seem to be getting a bit better at inclusion, there is still a long, long way to go to address these issues.

Exclusionary practice. Some autism organisations have what I term legacy thinking, meaning that they once had a good message but now have outlived their usefulness. These are often the organisations which have no autistic representatives on their board or which promote "awareness" events that are exclusionary, such as "light it up blue". Organisations supporting autistic people really do need to be genuinely inclusive themselves.

Accessing healthcare is a nightmare for many autistic people and families. Health settings such as hospitals can be terrifying and exclusionary, and medical professionals can be ignorant about autism and do more harm than good. This situation is so bad that many of us elect not to access treatment even when we need it. At the very least, training for medical and psychiatric staff needs to include some autism training as part of accreditation and qualifications.

Gender diversity and sexuality are a significant consideration for many autistic people. However, attitudes around sexuality and gender diversity can be stuck in the Dark Ages a lot of the time, especially for Disabled people. Some believe that we are all cis gender and asexual or heterosexual. This goes across all the items listed here – in employment, education, healthcare, and so on. There needs to be much more advocacy and understanding in this space to ensure young people grow up safe, and autistic people are seen as who we are in terms of our whole identity, whatever that may be .

Media. Wider society has a lot to learn about autism and autistic experiences. Sensationalist pieces in news media and stereotypical autistic characters on television do nothing to help. We need more representation of autistic experience and also autistic characters in television dramas who are not white cis gender heterosexual middle-class men. Attitudes around disability and other differences need to be improved on a societal level too .

Ongoing ableism. I absolutely long for the day that I will not be needed as an advocate because we will have achieved all we need to. It is important to understand, though, that nothing is set in stone. This stuff is all up for grabs, making it so important to advocate and be a strong presence fighting ableism and discrimination. We don't know the future, but we can help shape it.

Advocacy

The struggle against ableism continues and that adds up to a lot of advocacy needed! Thankfully, there are now quite a lot of us working on these things. When I started, there were a handful of us in Australia and a few more overseas. But at this point in time, there are many autistic advocates and activists and also some genuine allies coming from a place of respect and listening, supporting this work.

Self-advocacy – for yourself! (Purkis, 2023)

I just finished delivering a course on advocacy for NDIS provider Feros Care. I spent eight weeks talking to a number of other autistic people about how to be an advocate. It was really lovely.

I never really think about advocating for myself, though. I do societal advocacy – I try to change the wider world for neurodivergent and Queer folks rather than changing my own world. Last weekend, I was in Adelaide for the last session of the Feros course. It was just lovely. One of the attendees told me her manager had noticed a difference in her and she told me it was because of the course that I had delivered. Talk about absolutely making my day!

When I got to the airport to go home, I was feeling pretty good. I had some food and went to the gate, where I was greeted with a bunch of very loud schoolkids, also going to Canberra. This was a bit of a sensory assault and then the flight was delayed. I went from being a happy Yennski to being a very stressed Yennski.

Finally, we were allowed to board the plane. The flight attendant announced this over the loudspeaker and, as they always do, asked anyone who needed to board first, to come to the counter. For the first time in my life, I approached and said, "I am autistic and have schizophrenia, and the kids are bothering me with their noise". Not only had I never done this, but it had never occurred to me that I could do it! The flight attendant was lovely and said how she was having issues with the kids' noise too so couldn't imagine how challenging it must be for me. She also got me a seat on the plane away from the kids. I was delighted.

After this, I reflected on what had happened. I had used my assertiveness and advocacy skills to support myself for once and it had gone really well. Of course, it could have gone differently as not everyone is inclusive, but it was such a positive experience, and it demonstrated that I can advocate for myself as well as try to change the world.

I think I have learned from this experience. I put the story on social media and had lots of positive responses. One person said, "thank you for leading by example". I hadn't thought that me supporting myself would also support other people! It was a sort of win-win. It took a long time for me to be able to do what I did. I have viewed myself as an advocate for almost 20 years, but it took me that long to confidently practice what I preach!

I will now do similar things to get my needs met if I need to. It was an empowering thing to do. I tend to be a person who doesn't want to "bother" anyone when it comes to my own experience, so I will often fix myself rather than trying to fix the situation, which is odd as I do not take that approach if someone else is having a tough time. In that situation, I would stand up for others – either individuals or in society – but I don't generally stand up for myself. I am hoping my recent experience means I will stand up for myself more often. It was certainly quite liberating and it made me feel good.

Resilience

Resilience is something of a fraught concept, especially in the neurodivergent community. People are told they should "get some resilience", which is often used as an excuse for blaming the victim of bullying. I have been talking about resilience for over ten years and it is probably the most misunderstood concept that I speak on. The blog posts here on resilience unpack what I mean when I say resilience and why many people struggle with it. I want a world where people have a better understanding of resilience and why it is important, and where autistic and neurodivergent folks more generally are able to make use of resilience.

Why I talk about autism and resilience so much (Purkis, 2017)

In 2012, I met an autistic young man. We will call him Adam. Anyone who has been to one of my talks on employment, education, or resilience will probably have heard this story. When I told Adam I am autistic, work full-time in Government administration, and – at that point – had one published book, he said, "You're lying. That isn't possible". I was keen to defend my integrity but then realised that in Adam's world at least, an autistic person couldn't do those things. Adam and his parents had been given a deficits-based view of what autism means, and it was clear Adam had not been allowed to undertake all that many things which challenged him. At age 21, he had a year nine education and had not engaged in any study in the preceding six years. He had gone onto the disability pension as soon as he was eligible, at the age of 16. I saw Adam and felt for him. I thought that he had been done a big disservice by all the deficits thinking, the fear that if something was hard, he would be upset or have a meltdown, which must be avoided at all costs.

It was almost as though the things which had been done with the intention of caring for him and making his life more pleasant as a child had in fact backfired. At the time I met Adam, I had always believed that an early autism diagnosis was a positive thing, helping autistic young people know their identity and get the supports they needed to navigate the world. But the world Adam navigated was his bedroom and the virtual worlds in online games. I do not criticise Adam and I know that life is complicated and people can struggle to engage with the world for a number of reasons. All I knew was that I wanted to help create a world in which autistic young people could be proud of who they are and take on and overcome the challenges they need to engage in life in the best way for them. At that moment of realisation, my work in advocacy began in earnest.

I interpreted the main issues Adam was facing were due to a lack of being allowed to take on challenges and risks and to be supported through those. The primary issue in my mind was that a lack of capacity for resilience was holding people like Adam back. This became a big motivator for me and still is what drives my passion. My *Wonderful World of Work* book was written as a direct means of addressing the issues I saw around resilience and autism.

Resilience to me is about being able to take on challenges, work through them, and come out the other side with confidence and mastery, and that confidence and mastery can translate across and into other challenges and areas of life. This is not a quick process and it does not stand alone. Things like self-esteem, confidence, and independence are all related to resilience.

One thing to clear up about resilience, though. When someone tells me that – usually an educator – has told them their autistic child will not be bullied if they "get some resilience", it makes my blood boil. The person saying that is not speaking about resilience or anything close to it. What they are doing is dismissing and invaliding that child's experience; they are blaming the victim. No matter how a child became a bully, the victim of that bully's poor behaviour is not responsible for the bullying behaviour in any way. That is NOT resilience. Genuine resilience has a range of benefits to autistic children and adults.

I am interested in this topic for a number of reasons in addition to Adam. One of them is that I used a process of controlled challenges[3] to build my own capacity to work after being outside the labour force for almost ten years in my early adult life. I didn't articulate or understand that I was "doing resilience" and it was quite intuitive – it just seemed like a good approach at the time! I went from having a severe experience of perfectionism at a dishwashing job resulting in mental health issues requiring hospitalisation. My issue was the perceived level of responsibility at work. Even though the worst mistake I could make in the dishwashing job would probably be to send a dirty fork out, in my mind if I screwed up, the whole business would go broke.

At the time this happened, I didn't for one moment think I would never be able to work, despite that seeming the likely outcome of my problematic work history. Instead, I thought, "I can't work now, at this moment in time". In the next five years, I built my work resilience by working as a volunteer in a gallery, building confidence from that to having a very small business doing video editing for my art school colleagues, developing confidence from that to work in a charity, and then after six months of that and the publication of my first book, moving on to a full-time professional role. I had built my resilience for work from being terrified of the tiniest amount of responsibility to working in a corporate role with lots of responsibility. I have been in my corporate workplace for almost 11 years now and have even more responsibility at work and in my advocacy work too. I rarely think about the responsibly, just do what I need to do.

This should be seen in the context of challenges faced by autistic people in completing study and finding work. The example above illustrates how I managed my individual issues regarding work through resilience. However, there are also broader social issues and disadvantages which my getting a job didn't and couldn't overcome. Addressing these issues does require a broader approach than expecting individual autistic people to work through their individual challenges.

And there is a bit of an ulterior motive for this post. (Cue shameless book plug!) My friend, colleague, and co-author, Dr Emma Goodall, and I have written two books for parents to support their autistic kids aged 2–10 to build resilience, and a book for parents of kids and young people aged 11–20 years. These books are really practical and written from a strengths-based perspective. This means that commentary around autism and the capability of autistic people is based on capability rather than solely based on what they cannot achieve or their deficits. The focus is on understanding and supporting autistic kids to navigate the world and become fulfilled adults reaching their own potential, whatever that may mean for them.

Failing successfully (Purkis, 2021)

I wrote two books on resilience for parents of autistic kids with my wonderful co-author, Dr Emma Goodall, in 2017 and 2018. When we pitched the books to my publisher, we gave some chapter examples including one on "failing successfully". The publisher loved this idea, and we got a contract. Failing successfully is a concept I have been talking about for a while, mostly because – similarly to many other autistic people – I really struggle with mistakes, setbacks, and failure.

Less than a week ago, I made a mistake. This is what prompted this post as I wanted to connect with others who also struggle with worry around mistakes and failure. My mistake revolved around not adequately de-identifying some people that I said I had issues with. A friend of one of the people contacted me and explained that the examples were not adequately de-identified as she could make out who one of them was. Apparently, the person themselves could work out who they were. It was an absolute disaster! Of course, I took down the post and rewrote it minus the examples, and hopefully nothing untoward happened after that, but I was absolutely horrified. I felt guilty for being part of the problem rather than part of the solution – even though it was unintentional. I imagined how I would feel if someone posted negative comments about me, and I worried that it would escalate and I would have legal issues. As a perfectionist, making a mistake is always difficult.

However, when I unpacked it, this incident actually had some elements which were quite useful, the main one being that I learned from it. If I am describing anyone in writing in unfavourable terms, I am very careful not to add any identifying features. In fact, I check everything I write that references others very carefully to ensure that I am not inadvertently criticising anyone or being disrespectful. These are good learnings and an example of what I see as "successful failure". Something unpleasant had happened which was my fault, but I immediately worked to rectify the issue and I have learned some useful lessons from it which will improve my work in the future and avoid the same issue happening again. So, while it was very stressful and I felt extremely guilty, it can also be seen as a success.

As autistic people, we often struggle with perfectionism and fear of failure. The anxiety related to this can mean we don't do things which we would actually enjoy or do well. Perfectionism can stop us in our tracks. I knew somebody at university who wrote an amazing essay but didn't hand it in until it was vastly overdue because it wasn't perfect. Had she handed it in on time, I imagine she would have gained a high distinction, but she had to keep working on it to make it perfect. By the time she submitted it, it was so overdue that she barely scraped a pass despite it being a stunning piece of writing. I have similar reflections from my own life but in relation to employment. In 2001, I got a dishwashing job and was so anxious about potentially making a mistake that the anxiety triggered a psychotic episode. I was unable to work again for years and had to instigate a series of controlled challenges around employment in order to work at all. Controlled challenges is part of building resilience and involves putting in place incrementally more challenging tasks or activities in order to build confidence and competence.

The worry about making a mistake can absolutely defeat us. The successful failing model is not about saying it is OK to make mistakes with consequences, or that it doesn't matter if you make a mistake. Often it DOES matter. However, the successful failing model is all about using experiences of failure and setbacks to build an understanding which will help you avoid the same issue in the future. It is also about building your confidence and resilience. It can be soul-destroying to make an error if you dwell on it and just feel guilty. Seeing errors differently and as a learning experience, and seeing setbacks as an inevitable part of life at times is a far better approach.

The key is to reflect on the fact that everyone makes mistakes, that mistakes can foster learning and understanding, and that you can use the learnings from a mistake to improve how you approach things in the future. Autistic people in particular tend to need this skill as we often struggle a lot with perfectionism and anxiety around errors. It is possible to instil this understanding in autistic kids as well. I wish I had the knowledge of successful failing as a kid and a young adult.

Allies

Allyship is something which has been raised a lot in recent times, but allies have been around forever. An ally is someone who supports people from an inclusion-type group but who is not a member of that group themselves (Reframing Autism, 2023). A good ally is a good thing to have . Recently, we have been viewing allyship through the context of intersectionality, which I think is often a very helpful approach. The concept of intersectionality describes the ways in which systems of inequality based on gender, race, ethnicity, sexual orientation, gender identity, disability, class, and other forms of discrimination "intersect" to create unique dynamics and effects (Centre for Intersectional Justice, 2023). Through this lens, an ally is a privileged person supporting someone who lacks privilege themselves. Pretty much anyone who belongs to one or another privileged group can be an ally. I think the world in general would benefit from greater understanding of intersectionality. I want to see more allies in the future and for people to have confidence to be allies. Sometimes people are anxious around being criticised as allies or "getting it wrong" and inadvertently offending someone. It is important to support allies in their allyship and reassure them and affirm them when they do the right thing.

All about allies (Purkis, 2021)

I recently finished writing a book on advocacy with my co-author, the awesome Barb Cook. The book is all about how to advocate for neurodivergent people. One thing we covered was allies.

What is an ally? A quick Google search came up with this definition: *To be an ally is to unite oneself with another to promote a common interest.* As shown by the definition above, people who are allies are not only helpers, but also have a common interest with those they desire to help. In an alliance, both parties stand to benefit from the bond or connection they share.

So, what makes an ally? A good ally has the interests of the person they are supporting at heart and recognises that they are not being an ally for their own interests but for the interests of the person they are supporting. A good ally does not make it all about themselves. A good ally listens and provides support and encouragement.

Lots of groups have allies – for example, straight allies are very common in the LGBTQA+ community. In the autism advocacy space, there are also a lot of allies. Often, allistic parents will advocate on behalf of – or together with – their autistic kids.

Some allies and ways of being an ally are problematic. When allistic people ignore or even go against the needs and wants of the autistic person they are "supporting", this is a problem. Any kind of co-advocacy or of speaking on behalf of, needs to put the needs and wants of the autistic person to the front and centre even if the autistic person is a child. This is particularly the case if the autistic person is a child! Children often can't advocate for themselves, so they need an ally to support them in getting their needs met. This is fine but the allyship must be inclusive, or it is possible that it will be discriminatory and unhelpful.

I regularly post memes on social media relating to different elements of life as a neurodivergent person. I used to call them memes, but was criticised for this as they aren't necessarily funny – which apparently memes are supposed to be! To address this, I started calling them Yemes as nobody can criticise me for that! I publish them weekly, and they cover a large range of topics. I remember posting a Yeme once which basically said allistic people should not speak on behalf of autistics. I got a lot of negative feedback on this, mostly from parents. In this instance, the criticism was probably justified. There are situations where allistic people – especially parents and carers – will need to speak on behalf of an autistic person, often a child. Speaking on behalf of someone doesn't always have to be negative, but it really, really needs to be inclusive . If you are advocating for an autistic child as an ally, make sure where possible that you communicate with them as to their needs and wants prior to the advocacy. And a person does not need to have verbal speech to communicate. If you are caring for someone who does not use verbal speech, then make sure you get an alternative and augmented communication (AAC) device for them. There are so many ways a person can communicate that don't involve spoken words. Communication is absolutely the key to advocacy, and a person who is denied the ability to communicate is likely to be very frustrated and will struggle to get their needs met.

The area of allies and representing the needs of autistic people is a challenging one. Some people who claim to be allies are in fact doing more harm than good. An ally needs to have respect, understanding, and acceptance of the autistic person they are being an ally for. They need to listen, and they need to ensure their allyship is genuine and based strongly in the needs of the autistic person they are supporting.

When I was a kid, we had an integration aide at my school. This woman was just awful. She was repeatedly mean to me, including asking if my mum cut my hair – apparently being poor is a reason to criticise a child. This woman was supposed to be a support person for kids with disabilities, but she was really unpleasant and rude to at least one Disabled kid – me. This person was hired in a role where she was supposed to essentially be an ally, but she was very poor at the role and was harmful and rude. Allyship is such an important thing, and it needs to be done well and with a lot of respect and kindness, not judgement or selfishness.

A good ally can make a huge difference, and an unhelpful ally can do just the opposite. If you are an ally, please consider your role and think about how you can genuinely support autistic people to reach our potential and navigate the world well. Allies can be an effective support in difficult situations, and for people who struggle to advocate for themselves, they can be the change and the difference that is required. One thing I would say to all allies is "remember it is not about you". And a big thank you genuine allies for making the world a better place for so many of us.

Conclusion

Advocacy and allyship are extremely important things for autistic people – kids and adults alike. Self-advocacy can make a difference for autistic people. Encouraging self-confidence, allyship, assertiveness, and resilience can be instrumental in improving life for autistic people. Resilience is about promoting confidence, self-esteem, and using experience to build a sense of pride. It is not about blaming the victim, putting the onus on autistic people for the poor behaviour of others. Having a sense of confidence and resilience, being able to self-advocate, and having allies and genuine supporters from the allistic and neurotypical communities can make a big difference and promote autistic thriving.

4
Navigating the social world

The wider world can be quite confusing and upsetting for autistic people. We can struggle to be socially accepted, and things like work and education can be difficult for us to navigate. Assumptions around our communication and how we socialise can make life difficult. It is important to promote the idea that autistic communication and socialising – including things like expressing empathy, feeling the need to mask in order to be socially accepted, and managing relationships with friends can either be empowering and positive, or not.

Autistic people are often criticised or misunderstood for our communication. We tend to communicate differently to our neurotypical peers. Differences can include using idioms, taking literal approaches to the world, being scrupulously honest – even when we don't really mean to – and differences around non-verbal communication such as facial expression, body language, and eye contact (Reframing Autism, 2023). Autistic people can communicate in a way that is often misinterpreted by their neurotypical peers, leading to confusion. It can be highly frustrating for autistic people to make themselves understood to neurotypical and allistic folks – and vice versa! Autistic ways of communicating are often viewed as "wrong". Children are given therapies such as Applied Behaviour Analysis to help them appear somehow more neurotypical in their presentation and communication. These kinds of therapies often come from the position of autistic communication being somehow wrong and in need of fixing (Kupferstein, 2018).

To my mind, autistic communication is perfectly valid but different. When I started my advocacy journey in 2005, the prevailing view seemed to be that of trying to "fix" autistic people. Thankfully, things are changing in the space, and the more inclusive models of understanding communication such as viewed through the social model of disability and the human rights model seem more popular and common.

Autistic culture and communication – learning to speak autistic (Purkis, 2021)

I came upon the realisation of an idea a while back – that of "autistic culture". I wasn't the first person to talk about this, but it was an epiphany when I came to the realisation that such a thing exists.

To illustrate this, let me get in my metaphorical TARDIS and go back in time to 2005… I had just had my first book accepted for publication and was finding my way around the autistic community – or the part of the autistic community which lived in Melbourne and congregated around author and advocate Polly Samuel. I hadn't been in touch with many autistic people prior to meeting Polly and suddenly I found myself surrounded by fellow autistics. I noticed a few things about my new peer group.

The first was that we were all very many individuals. The second was that there were two main approaches people took to understanding our communication differences from others. The first group said something along the lines of "People don't like me or understand me. What am I doing wrong?" And the second group said, "People don't like or understand me. They must be idiots!" I was definitely in the first group, but it got me thinking about communication and understanding across neurotypes.

It also got me thinking about how we interpret the world and our place in it as neurodivergent folks. I figured that we could view being autistic as like being residents in a strange country where the locals don't speak our language. We learn some words in the local language, but it never comes naturally and we long for our fellow expats. The cultural model goes further than this. If we imagine autistic people as being French speakers, and neurotypical folks as being German speakers, this gives us a lens through which to understand communication across neurotypes. It is not that the neurotypical "German speakers" understand that we usually speak French and that because of this our "German" isn't so fluent. It is more that the neurotypical German speakers don't even understand that there is a French language. Neurotypical people frequently have no understanding of neurodiversity and simply assume autistic folks are inept at communicating.

It is actually not the case that autistic people communicate poorly. We don't. We communicate very well but just differently. Prior to the Covid-19 pandemic, I often attended big autism conferences. There was a quiet room at these events. If you went into the quiet room during the lunch break, you would see a group of people having a fantastic conversation. The people would all understand each other and know where each other was coming from. The people in this group were all autistic. Social skills and communication were going on very well, and if a neurotypical person entered, then they would be at a disadvantage in terms of their communication. Autistics don't communicate badly; we simply communicate differently. Put a bunch of us together and you will see that communication at work. Our "French" is perfectly fine, and we can understand each other. Just because autistics don't communicate like neurotypicals does not mean we cannot communicate.

The cultural model of autism allows for greater respect and inclusion. It is also more accurate than saying we communicate badly, lack empathy, or have poor social skills. There is a lot of time, money, and effort spent trying to make autistic people seem more neurotypical. Not only is this unhelpful, but it can actually be traumatising for autistic people, and it doesn't really achieve anything. Autistic people are not communicating badly; rather, we are just communicating differently. This model is one of inclusion, which enables us to understand the value of autistic people. It also makes it easier to communicate with us and understand we are different, not less.

Autistic people are constantly being encouraged – and sometimes coerced – to seem less autistic and more neurotypical. In the not-so-distant past, left-handed kids were forced to write with their right hand. We now understand that this is unhelpful and damaging for those kids. Could we maybe do the same with autistic communication? Autistics are speaking another language – a language which is valid and beautiful and perfectly

OK. So rather than forcing autistic people to "speak neurotypical", maybe people could learn to speak Autistic? That would be so good.

Empathy

Perceptions around empathy and autism have changed immensely in my almost 20 years as an advocate. I remember being told that autistic people lacked "theory of mind" (Baron-Cohen, 1985), and we couldn't understand or relate to others because we lacked the ability to see things from others' perspective. There was a model called the Sally Anne experiment which posited that autistic people cannot empathise with others as they do not have the ability to perceive life through someone's else's viewpoint. I remember thinking when I first came across this idea that nobody can tell what another person is thinking, autistic or otherwise. The lack of theory of mind was not an autistic experience; it was probably a universal one!

Thankfully, in recent years the understanding of empathy and autism has evolved. Autistic academics and thinkers such as Dr Damian Milton and Dr Wenn Lawson have approached the issue of empathy from a more inclusive view. The idea of object permanence and the "double empathy problem" have helped challenge this unhelpful view around autistic people lacking empathy (Milton, 2022).

The double empathy problem revolves around the idea that autistic people and neurotypical people approach empathy differently and as such find it hard to empathise with one another (Milton, 2022). Neurotypical people observing autistic people assume they lack empathy when, in fact, they do not empathise in the same way a neurotypical person does. Likewise, autistic people think neurotypical / allistic people are lacking in empathy. In fact, neither group lacks empathy – they just it differently. The reason autistic people are blamed for lacking empathy seems to me to be more related to us being the minority than much else. These views from Drs Milton and Lawson are becoming more commonly accepted even among neurotypical researchers and clinicians. To my mind, they offer a more inclusive and accurate explanation of the issue.

Why empathy is not as simple as it seems (Purkis, 2022)

I recently posted a meme about the myth that autistic people lack empathy. I said that it is not true that we lack empathy and to say so was unhelpful and damaging. I got some interesting responses to this post, including a few from autistic people saying they have low or no empathy. This got me thinking about my own experiences and has led to my feeling the need to unpack the idea of empathy and autism as it is possibly more complex than dismissing the experience of those who have low or no empathy.

When I was younger, I always thought I had no empathy. I didn't feel sad when other people were having a hard time. If someone died, they were simply not in my life any more and I accepted that. I didn't understand the consequences of my actions. So, while I didn't want to hurt anyone, if I did, then I would not feel much remorse. However, I also had the ability to take on the same emotions of those around me as if by osmosis. I now care immensely and want to ensure everyone I interact with is feeling happy and doing well. I worry about friends and am very sensitive to the moods of those around me.

All of this paints a picture of quite a complex experience of empathy. I am at once lacking in empathy, experiencing hyper-empathy and experiencing what I would call practical empathy (empathy from a logical, "thinking" perspective without an emotive component). I imagine that other autistic people share these experiences or their own versions of this.

One thing which always worried me was my struggle to grieve when anyone died. Death to me is inevitable, and when someone dies, they are no longer in your life. There is no way of contacting the person and they exist in your memory. As a child and young adult, I never grieved. I didn't know what it meant to grieve. When someone left the world, they left the world. I could not contact them, so I got on with life without them. I just felt a bit sad and wished there was a phone to heaven so I could tell them about my day! Dr Wenn Lawson talks about the concept of object permanence and autism rather than about people lacking empathy, and I agree with him on this. While I miss a friend or relative who has passed, they are no longer in my world and that is OK.

When I was younger, I struggled with aggression. I was upset and regretted my actions, but I didn't feel anything emotive about it. The way I overcame violence was through practical, logical thought. I met some people who were victims of violence and I saw how it had affected them. I did not want to be responsible for anyone feeling that way, so I stopped my aggressive behaviour. This is not empathy in the traditional sense. It is what I would call practical empathy. It also related to consequences. Understanding consequences was a major issue for me – maybe in a similar way to the object permanence issue, I think. Once I had figured out what the consequences of my actions were and that they were negative, I changed how I acted.

Empathy is a complex thing. It is not well understood. I think most autistic people that I have met have quite a lot of empathy of one sort or another. Even people who appear to lack empathy – like me in the past – may actually have quite a lot of it. It may seem that someone lacks empathy when in fact they express and experience it in different ways. I do think it is a harmful myth to say that autistic people lack empathy. The idea behind this myth came from a clinician in the UK, Simon Baron-Cohen (Baron-Cohen, 1985), some years ago, but it has remained a pervasive issue. It harms autistic people to be told we lack empathy – especially for people who have lots of it and those who experience it differently to others. This is another area where greater understanding about autism is essential.

In my own life it has been the case that I struggled with consequences for some years and with emotional empathy, but that I also have a lot of the kind of empathy where I can pick up on the moods of others as if by osmosis. In recent years I have gained a lot of practical empathy. Practical empathy is where a person does kind things and supports others in practical ways rather than through an emotional connection. I have immense amounts of practical empathy. It drives my advocacy work and writing. So, while I don't grieve much when someone passes, I do a whole range of things to demonstrate that I care for others.

Empathy is more complicated than it is often portrayed. So, there are some autistic people who are highly empathetic in different ways, some who are empathic in some ways and not others (like me), and some who have low or no empathy. This isn't just the case for autistic people. Some neurotypical people also fit these descriptions. Levels and experiences of empathy are not right or wrong; they just are and that is OK and not a reason for criticism or judgement.

Relationships and friends

I think everyone finds friendships and relationships tricky, but for autistic folks it can be particularly so. The assumption is often that autistic people lack social skills and the ability to be a good friend or partner, but this is not necessarily the case (Wang, 2009). Autistic people often thrive when among other autistic or otherwise neurodivergent people, and these can be lasting friendships or relationships. This is not to say that autistic people cannot have friends and partners from among neurotypical or allistic people.

Often, social communication with allistic and neurotypical people can be exhausting. People may feel the need to mask and pretend to be different in order to be socially accepted in neurotypical circles. This can also mean people are thought to be coping really well so they don't need any support! Some autistic people are so adept at masking that they believe themselves to be whatever identity they are trying to be!

A few years back, there was a campaign in the autistic community called "Take the mask off" (Reframing Autism, 2023). This was to my mind a positive thing, but it raised some other questions such as, what if you have been masking so long that you don't know how to take the mask off? What if your job or even your partner expects the version of you that you have always presented? You might worry about not being accepted as your true self – and this worry may actually be well founded. It is not simply enough to tell people to take the mask off. We need to put in place supports and promote inclusion so that people actually feel free to be their true self.

My starring role – autism and masking (Purkis, 2018)

When I was a teenager, I was very unpopular and bullied a lot at school. I worked out almost as soon as I started high school that there was something about me that separated me from my peers. I knew I was "different" for the first time when I was 11. I didn't want this difference. It meant people ostracised and ridiculed me. I wanted to be like the other kids, but I couldn't figure out how. I thought my English accent as a newly arrived "pommie" (as my classmates called me) was the reason that others found me different, so I set about becoming as Australian sounding as I could. That didn't work, so I changed my dress sense to what I thought was generic and nondescript, once again without success. I really couldn't work out to how be more socially acceptable, so I changed how I spelled my name – thinking being "Janette" would make me more popular than "Jeanette". Of course, that didn't work either.

The chameleon-like qualities I discovered in my early high school years became more finely honed as I reach adulthood. However, the only groups I could successfully blend in with and be accepted by were always negative and/or dangerous ones – criminals and people with drug and alcohol addiction issues. I was "acting" or "masking" my true self, with varying levels of conscious knowledge of it, until I was at least 30 years old.

My autism diagnosis was gained at age 20 and I had some vague awareness that fitting in, and masking was a "thing" related to autism, but I had difficulty accepting my autism, so didn't apply it to me. I could effortlessly slip into whatever character I thought I needed to. It was effective as long as my worlds didn't collide. I remember taking a call from one of my university lecturers while I was living in public housing when one of my very down-to-earth neighbours was visiting. He kept saying I must be a liar to be two people at the same time. It bothered him which was the "real" me. In fact, I don't think either was the "real" me, although my preference was probably the university "me". I was confused by this as I hadn't known anyone else witness my social chameleon figuratively trying to turn glitter purple and grey at the same time! I wondered if I was a liar, but now, I think it was a survival mechanism and not something I was conscious of at the time.

For me, and I imagine many other autistic people, my "masking" was a complex thing, borne out of a need to be socially accepted. Life seemed easier when I was masking. People tended to be more friendly and less hostile. Even if I had no idea what was happening in a conversation or relationship, I could at least escape being judged or ostracised by using the language and expression I knew were expected. Well, for a lot of the time anyway.

I actually became so adept at masking in my twenties that I believed I genuinely belonged to my adopted social group at the time, drug addicts and criminals. When I decided to remove myself from that very destructive culture, I didn't know who I was. I had been playing the druggie Jeanette role for almost five years. I didn't understand about masking and autism, but I understood that if I kept being the version of me I was at the time, I would not be around for much longer. I decided very clearly to change my life, and a changed life meant a changed me. I considered what I wanted my character to include and set about creating it. It involved a further kind of masking but perhaps a more helpful one. I was like an author creating parameters for a character in their novel, but the author and the character were both me.

My issue was always social acceptance: I craved it. I was desperate to belong to the extent that I didn't care what I did or said to be accepted. Being disliked, bullied, and hated at school left me with little or no self-esteem. I disliked myself. Learning to like myself again took many years, many accomplishments, and a lot of support from the few caring people in my life at the time, mostly my parents. I often find myself criticising that younger Jeanette for choosing a damaging peer group, but when I reflect that while I had a choice, I know it is not as simple as that.

I use masking as a coping strategy on occasion even now, and I think a lot of people do. The difficulties I have when people need to mask is not due to their actions, but in the reasons behind the masking and some of the responses to it which tend to happen from others, including the following:

- It costs someone their sense of identity – as it did for me. They can lose their sense of who they are, almost as if they are a spy terrified of their cover being blown.

- Clinicians sometimes use masking and acting in autistic people as a justification for misdiagnosis, saying they are "too social" or "managing too well to be autistic".
- If it is not understood that masking is happening, then the person who is masking as a coping strategy and going through trauma may not get assistance as they are seen to be managing.
- It is often discussed as only within the domain of autistic women and not men or gender-divergent autistics, which can impact on the support they receive, including misdiagnosis.
- It is viewed as intentional dishonesty or a character flaw.

In my experience and understanding, masking tends to be a social survival strategy. The key to addressing it is to address the reasons that such a survival strategy is needed in the first place. In a world where neurodivergence was understood and respected, where autistic and other neurodivergent people were valued for what we bring to the world rather than expected to conform socially in order to be accepted … I reckon in that world masking would be a lot less necessary. So, let's work to create that world and along the way support autistic people to be proud of who we are and comfortable in our skin.

My ex-friends – learning it is OK not to be 100 per cent popular (Purkis, 2021)

Preface: I published this yesterday and included examples of toxic friendships. I thought they were nicely de-identified but apparently not, as someone identified one of them from my description. I immediately took the post down based on this experience. I apologise to anyone I may have upset or offended with the original version. Even if people treated me badly in the past, it is not OK for me to treat others badly myself. Thank you to the person who brought this to my attention. This revised version has no details of any individual, de-identified or otherwise.

I have a long list of people who used to be my friends but aren't any more. They range from people who have simply dropped off the list to those who actively hate me. I have people who have excised me from their lives, and people I have felt the need to excise from my own. Some of them I am very glad are gone. Removing a toxic person from your world is like being Frodo Baggins in *Lord of the Rings* when the ring gets destroyed. In the movie version, Frodo says, "It's gone!" with a huge sense of relief. That is definitely how I have felt when some people have gone from my world.

I have learned a lot from my experience with a number of toxic friends over the years. The most useful lesson was that it is OK to excise a person from your life. You do not need friendships which cause you only stress and misery. Now I am better at spotting the signs of a toxic narcissist, so hopefully I can avoid entering into friendships with these sorts of people in the first place.

One thing which has always worried me is when friends distance themselves from me and don't tell me the reason. I have had a few friends do this over the years and it always stresses me out. What did I do wrong? I wonder. Why does this person I used to be close with now not like me? I think that if a friend upsets you – and especially if they are autistic – it is best to tell them what the problem is. Not only will this avoid their being worried about what they did and ruminating on this and feeling bad about themselves, but it will also give you the opportunity to work out any differences and repair the relationship. It is always best to tell someone if there is an issue, but I recognise it can be difficult, especially for people who struggle with assertiveness.

One issue with ex-friends is when you encounter them unexpectedly and there is a very difficult exchange. This has happened to me a few times, most of which were extremely stressful and upsetting. I have improved in handling these situations, and on one occasion I managed to respond to the ex-friend with assertiveness, which was wonderful. Ten points to Yennski for assertiveness! It was a really difficult thing to do, but I feel like it was good to communicate clearly and stand up for myself.

These days I don't really care if I have a list of people who really dislike me, but in the past, this would have been a huge issue for me. I was bullied through school and had a number of traumatic experiences of abuse and violence as a young adult. I also spent time in prison where being a social outcast could result in some pretty dire situations including being attacked or killed. As a result of these texperiences, I longed for social acceptance, and any friendship was a good one in my book – the very notion of somebody not liking me or of my excising a friend from my life was unimaginable, and I had a lot of very unpleasant friendships as a result. As I grew older, I started to value and respect myself more. I realised that not everyone had to like me and if someone didn't like me, well, it was their loss! I am supremely unconcerned that I have enemies. As long as they don't hurt me, troll me, or attack me, they can hate me as much as they like. On a related point, when I started out as an advocate, I was terrified of bad press and criticism. I would be anxious every time I posted a blog, in case I upset anyone. Now I can look at a one-star review of my books and not be particularly bothered by it. This change in attitudes is an absolute liberation.

I think a lot of people who have experienced bullying and other abuse can struggle with these sorts of issues. This is true for a lot of autistic people. It is great to get a place where you don't really care, and you are confident and comfortable enough in yourself to let people go who are not really acting like friends, and to not worry so much if someone "dumps" you.

The autistic community and autistic space

When I started out as an advocate, the idea of an autistic community was in its infancy. The term "neurodiversity" was coined in the 1990s, and the Autistic Self-Advocacy Network was campaigning for inclusion and respect at the same time, but I didn't realise there was an actual defined autistic community until the late 2000s.

When I started out as an advocate, autism was mostly viewed as a deficit and a negative. I remember being horrified by the attitudes of some parents and clinicians and service providers who seemed to think autism was a tragedy. Autistic children in particular were often viewed as a burden.

It wasn't until much later that I realised that autistic people had a community. I think social media has played a large role in this and also that advocates were getting more of an audience for their message. I didn't know about autistic space until relatively recently. Autistic space is where everyone in a group is autistic. It may happen briefly – such as at a conference in the sensory room – or over a more prolonged period. Autistic space is amazing, and some of my absolute all-time favourite experiences have taken place in autistic space. One was at a research co-design workshop organised by the Autism Cooperative Research Centre; another was at a weekend escape to the country to a spa resort with all autistic women and gender-divergent folks; and more recently it was in a course that I ran on advice for a disability services provider. If I were in autistic space every day, I think I would probably be 100 per cent happy! I wish my whole life were lived in autistic space! I also wish that we were routinely understood and respected so that autistic space was not such a stark contrast from the neurotypical space that we spend the vast majority of our lives inhabiting.

We are family – autistic space (Purkis, 2019)

Last week, I had what could only be described as a silly schedule. Four states and four events in five days. Lots of people expressed concern about the impact of all this busyness on my admittedly "interesting" mental health. However, I wasn't too worried because I knew that I would be with autistic friends and colleagues for most of the time and it would be empowering rather than draining. I was correct, and all the events were positive and energising, mostly due to lots of my autistic friends and peers being in attendance.

I love autism events, but not so much because of the event but because of the attendees. There are quite a few people who attend these things who I love spending time with. Autism world events attended by actually autistic people are a bit addictive! Being around "family" or "tribe" or however you put it, is one of the best things ever.

When I am around my autistic peers, I can be entirely myself. I am understood, and I understand them. There is no worrying about subtext and hidden meanings in conversations. There is no worrying that I will be taken advantage of and tricked into doing something I don't want to. There is a lot of shared experience and wonderful friendships.

Being with autistic people in a group is one of my favourite things. That "autistic space" where we get to be around others who are like us and who "get" us is magical. Autistic space is something I have only experienced a few times. It is where everyone is autistic, and autists are managing things and making the decisions. It is wonderful and empowering.

The idea of autistic space is related to a few things – autistic pride, the neurodiversity movement, and the idea of "different not less", but it also relates to that wonderful concept of autistic culture. I have been talking about autistic culture for a while now and I think the idea has stuck – well, I hope it has! Autistic culture is based in the way autistic people generally communicate differently to allistic people. Our communication is not "wrong" or broken; rather, it is just different. So, if an autistic person is in a roomful of allistic people, then they will struggle with communication. But if this is reversed, an allistic person will struggle to be understood in a room full of autistics.

It often feels to me like I am an expatriate in another country. I have learned the language and some of the customs, but I am not at home. When I meet another expat from the land of Aut, I am delighted as they know my country. We talk and relate our experiences of being in the strange land of the allistics and there is fellow feeling as we are of the same culture. My love of autistic space comes down to that. Autistic space is like a visit to our homeland. It is hard to leave autistic space. I often reflect that I would like to live in autistic space permanently.

The thing about being among autistic "family" is that it replenishes my energy and my mental health and well-being. I am not alone in this. Other autistics who have spent time in autistic space long to do so again. I have been wondering if there is a way to create autistic space which would last almost all the time. A community of autistics living and working together. A very nice idea but not something I have the skills or funding to realise. It would be amazing to have such a place.

I think the takeaway from these musings is that knowing your tribe, your family is a vital part of autistic people's lives – it's very lonely in a foreign country where nobody speaks your language, and this is infinitely improved by compatriots sharing a metaphorical drink and sharing stories of home.

Conclusion

There is no reason that autistic people cannot thrive, be included and accepted. While the world we live in is often not respectful of our experiences and differences, with a little more goodwill and understanding, life could be that much easier for those of us who are autistic. Some unhelpful views in the past have led to the idea that autistic people lack empathy, make poor friends, or are "weird". Not only is this inaccurate, but it is also disrespectful and ableist. We are different and that is OK. To me, neurotypical people are weird, but even so, some of my best friends are neurotypical!

Socialising and communication are things autistic people do just as well as our allistic and neurotypical peers – we just do them differently. A world where no autistic person needed to mask would be a good world and is certainly one that I aspire to help bring about. Attitudes around autistic communication are definitely changing, but more change needs to happen.

5
Gender diversity and sexuality

Autism and gender diversity – experiences of autistic folks, challenges, and empowerment

Research demonstrates that autistic people are significantly more likely to be trans and/or gender divergent than our neurotypical peers. This statistic is repeated across a large number of studies (Glaves et al., 2023).

The reasons for this are not entirely known but may be due to a number of factors, such as some autistic people not having a need to be considered socially acceptable and fit within a "norm" of gender. It may be the case that there are considerably more trans neurotypical people but that they are less able to come out than their more open autistic peers and remain closeted. There may be a separate neurotype of autistic and gender divergent, or it may be a combination of factors. It is possible that each autistic and gender-divergent person has a different range of factors contributing to their gender.

Divergent sexuality and gender diversity are not new things. The spectrum of human sexuality and human gender identity spans countless millennia and thousands of different cultures. It is important to remember that gender and sexuality are social constructs from particular cultural contexts. Many cultures on the planet have identities for gender outside the male/female binary (Urquhart, 2019).

Trans Day of Visibility (Purkis, 2023)

Yesterday, 31 March, was International Transgender Day of Visibility. I think this is a really important day. It was created to celebrate trans experience and promote pride. The other major transgender day is Transgender Day of Remembrance, which is more focused on mourning those we have lost due to violence and suicide. Trans Day of Visibility has a more celebratory focus and I think that is something we need as well.

As I mentioned in a previous blog post, there is quite a lot of hatred and transphobia around at the moment. The bigoted minority seems to be growing more vocal and getting traction for their horrible message of hatred. We all need to stand up on the side of good and right and inclusion. This is where events like Trans Day of Visibility are so important.

I always worry about complacency in this space. There is a view among some people that things will somehow just get progressively more inclusive until bigotry is a thing of the past. I can categorically say that isn't the case. There is no room for complacency. This doesn't mean that everyone has to protest or lobby every day. Different people show their support in different ways. For example, I am not a big protester these days, but I have a reach in the community through my writing and talks. As such I try to use that as a platform to hopefully counter the hatred which is so prevalent.

On a personal note, I find the hatred really upsetting. There are people out there who hate me simply because I exist as a trans person. The hatred can make you want to hide away, go into the closet, metaphorically close the door, and not tell anyone about your identity. What a horrible world that is. The hatred actually makes me want to be even more visible, so others feel supported and more able to come out themselves. I hate the closet. It is dark and scary and lonely. As trans people, we deserve love respect and understanding – just like everyone else does. We have the right to be out loud and proud.

Visibility is such an important thing. If you can't see it, you can't be it. For trans folks who have recently come to their identity, having strong, positive trans role models is a wonderful thing. Having people who refuse to be silenced by the bigots makes it harder for the bigots to spread their nasty message. It can be really hard, though, and I would never blame anyone for feeling unable to come out.

I love my trans identity. I am immensely proud to be who I am. When people attack me, I use it as an example of why bigotry is not OK rather than trying to make myself invisible. My world is an inclusive one, but I know that for so many trans people – especially kids and young people – they are isolated and cut off from their peers and communities. I really don't want that to be the case for anyone. I want a world where we can be proud of who we are and there is no audience for bigots.

I am Yenn. Affirming gender, affirming self (Purkis, 2019)

On Monday, I was at work, sitting at my desk when what I can only call a flash of inspiration hit me. In less than the time it took you to read the last sentence, I found my name and I knew my name was Yenn.

I think I'd better backtrack a bit. Last year, I publicly affirmed that I am non-binary gender. This has been an amazing time of self-discovery and reflection. My old name, Jeanette, is about as gender loaded as you can get. I have had conversations with a Queer friend called Bernadette, and we both concluded our names were quite strongly suggestive of the feminine. When I came out, I wondered if I should change my name. I started thinking about it, but nothing worked. I concluded that I would know when I knew. And I did. The only convincing I needed when "Yenn" popped into my brain on Monday was to see what it looked like written down. I tried it with an "e" on the end, which didn't look right. I tried it as "Yenn" and I knew I had found my name.

I considered where it had come from and realised it has a few "parents", thoughts-wise. The main thing I see is poetry. To yen in poetry means yearning, or as I see it, aspiration and personal reflection – both things I have a lot of experience of. It is also a little nod to my old Jeanette name, and it is quite individual. Written it looks strong and complete. Spoken it sounds confident and passionate. It might seem like a very quick decision, but it was the culmination of a lot of reflection over the past few months.

When I knew my name, I knew I also needed to tell friends. I sent a message to a bunch of close friends and emailed my parents. I said, "I will take this gradually…" and then realised I do not "do" gradual, so on my way home from work, I changed the title of my social media pages to Yenn Purkis and posted a message about why I had done this. I have experienced a lot of transphobia and trolling over the past few months, so I was caught between liberation at my new name and terror that people would attack me. Thankfully, I have not had any negative responses, and nobody unfriended me on social media that I am aware of, out of almost 10,000 people on Facebook and 5,000 on Twitter. On Monday, I spent the afternoon and evening in a state of joy.

Yesterday, I heard my name spoken for the first time, incidentally by author Graeme Simsion as I was part of a launch event for his new book. He said "Yenn" and then smiled and told me I didn't immediately look around! It takes a while, I think, given I am new to it as well.

I am fairly certain there will be people who will not like my new name due to its connectedness to my gender identity. There are quite a few transphobic bigots in the world, even in the autism world sadly. I have had people say, "I thought this page was about autism, not gender" and insist any commentary I make stay on the autism topic only. To me, though, gender diversity and autism are fairly clearly linked with so many of us being trans and gender diverse. This is not just my anecdotal evidence either. There is a lot of research evidence which demonstrates this too. I am here as an advocate for autistic and trans and gender-diverse people alike, and I would much rather be a visible gender-diverse person if that helps others who feel they cannot come out themselves and are experiencing bigotry or self-hatred and doubt.

I am becoming acutely aware of why it is referred to as "transition" and not change. I really, really wish I could make a decision about my identity and expression and magically everything would change that needs to, but it doesn't work like that. The legacy things – writings about a gender I no longer identify with, my name changing across documents and profiles, people using my pronouns – these things really get to me. I just want it all done now. Maybe the need to wait and change things more slowly than I want is what my mum would call "good for your soul". Not sure.

The response I have had to my new name has been overwhelmingly beautiful. People I don't know at an event telling me what a lovely name it is; a colleague at work that I came out to giving me a card which says, "this calls for confetti" and has a really meaningful message that she has written; my boss telling me I have her full support and being available should I need her despite being busy; the almost 500 people who liked or reacted to my Facebook post about my new name; all the people saying, "Hi Yenn!" and "Your name is beautiful; the organisations changing my name on their promotional material for upcoming talks. This affirmation is so overwhelmingly lovely and was not really expected. I keep expecting hatred and there is none, quite the opposite in fact. I really wish this were the case for everyone affirming gender.

So, I am a new me. My old Jeanette name never really fitted to my mind. It feels like I was wearing a big old coat that didn't quite fit right and was uncomfortable. But it never occurred to me to take it off until I did, and now, I am in a metaphorical jacket that fits just right and looks good to me and others, and allows me to move freely and express myself the way I want to.

I might say that these things do not come without doubts and insecurity and lots of questioning, but within that there is somehow a great certainty as well.

I like my new me. This was an important week for me, so I wanted to share it with you all as well.

Autism and sexuality

Sexuality and gender are different things, and not in any way linked. As such, considerations around sexuality for autistic people are likely to differ from those related to gender. There is a myth that all autistics are asexual. Research demonstrates that autistic people are more likely to be of marginalised sexuality than their neurotypical peers (George et al., 2017). This includes rates of asexuality but also being gay, lesbian, bi+, pansexual, and/or polyamorous. The myth around asexuality is likely due to the way autistic people are so frequently infantilised and seen as perennial children.

Consensual sex between adults can be viewed as a very positive thing regardless of the neurotype of the participants! The increasing focus on sexuality among Disabled folks is a good thing too. For example, a number of organisations, such as Safer Girls Safer Women in Australia, and advocates are working to enable funding for Disabled people to access the services of sex workers. As with anyone, safety and consent are essential in any sexual encounter. Some autistic people may be more prone to being taken advantage of by a partner or even abused by a stranger. I want to see a world where autistic people of all sexualities can have the opportunity to engage in consensual sex with a partner or partners who respect them, and for the taboos around disability and sex to be a thing of the past.

Autism and sexuality and relationships (Purkis, 2021)

There is a pervasive stereotype that all autistic people are asexual and single. In fact, there is a pervasive view that all Disabled people are asexual and single. These assumptions come straight out of ableism and are really unhelpful.

The idea that we are all asexual seems to come from the view that we are eternal children. This is far from the truth. A huge number of autistic people have partners and their own children. Some autistic people are asexual just as some people in society more broadly are asexual, but many autistic people have a sexual appetite and a partner or partners. A lot of autistic people are gay, lesbian, bi, pansexual, or polyamorous. People make assumptions that we might not be able to manage in a relationship or that autistic people don't make good partners. I think that autistic people are just as likely to be a bad – or for that matter a good – partner as anyone else.

Some people think that any sexual relationship with an autistic person is exploitative and that our neurotypical partners must be abusing us as we are so innocent and childlike and incapable of "real" relationships. Great big whopping UGH to that! Some people do exploit autistic people, but it is certainly not the case that all relationships between neurotypical and autistic people are exploitative.

Many autistic people choose a partner or partners who are also neurodivergent. These relationships can be very strong and inclusive as each partner is likely to "get" their partner. That being said, we have our differences too, and some autistic people can be predatory. Your neurotype does not determine whether you will be a good partner – or a good human being for that matter!

Sex itself can be different for autistics. Many of us have sensory issues around touch. This can make sex a bit challenging. The key to managing this rests upon being able to articulate what is and isn't OK and to convey that to your partner. While it can be challenging talking about these things, it is really important to do so to ensure you enjoy your sexual experiences. Everyone has the right to gratifying and enjoyable sex – if that is what they want, of course! I should note that there is a difference between having sensory issues around intimate touch and being asexual. Having sensory issues does not necessarily mean a person doesn't want sex at all.

You have probably heard the term "asexual", which relates to someone who does not want sexual activity. There is another term, which is "greysexual". This is a bit like the gender identity of Demi boy or Demi girl. A Demi boy or Demi girl is a gender-divergent person who feels a little bit masculine or a little bit feminine. Similarly, a greysexual person is a little bit sexual. Greysexual people may have sensory issues around sexual contact – or they may not. I think it is wonderful that we have all these descriptors for sexuality and gender too. It makes it a lot easier to find others who share our experience.

Sometimes autistic people's intentions are misinterpreted, and we are seen as being predatory when that is not our intent. This is a huge issue. I know I used this example recently, but I'll use it again. I heard a story about an autistic young man who was on a bus. He leaned over and stroked a woman's leg. He was not being a sexual predator at all. He was touching her silver stimmy stockings because he loved the look of them. Of course, the woman didn't know that and called the police. In her mind, some creepy pervert had just assaulted her. In terms of predatory behaviour, autistic people are, sadly, very likely to be on the receiving end. Teaching autistic kids and young adults about consent and bodily autonomy is really important because autistic people can be vulnerable to abuse. "Protecting" kids from discussions around sex is not a good idea as ignorance can result in being less able to protect oneself. And in your discussions with autistic kids, use clear, specific language around body parts and activities, not vague discussions like "don't let anyone touch you down there…" Sometimes autistic people think that if a person tells them something is going to happen, then they have to go along with that.

Sexuality and romantic attraction can be different things. Actually, gender identity, gender expression, sexuality, and romantic attraction are all separate, independent concepts. People often conflate these things, but they are all different and often independent of one another. I myself am asexual but have romantic attention to androgynous folks – and to policewomen for some reason! I am not looking for a relationship and have been single since 2004, but if the right person came along who was also asexual and whom I found romantically attractive, I would probably have a relationship with them.

On being asexual (Purkis, 2022)

I am asexual. This means that I do not enjoy or have any interest in sex. There are different identities within the asexual "umbrella". Some asexual people have a little interest in sex and others – like me – find it revolting.

Apparently, there is research showing that asexual people are the least likely of any of the LGBTQIA+ identities to be "out" (Stonewall, 2023). The stigma around asexuality is significant. Asexual people, or "Aces", are often seen as being sad and pathetic. The film *The 40-Year-Old Virgin* sums up this perspective. Not having sex is seen as sad or pathetic and that a person is somehow missing out.

It took me a long time to accept and embrace my asexuality. For many years, I believed I must be a lesbian. I had a sexual encounter with a man when I was 16 which wasn't entirely consensual. Because of this, I thought men were icky and women were, well, slightly less icky, so I figured I must be a lesbian. However, as a lesbian I still found sex revolting. I had relationships because I thought that was what you were supposed to do, but I didn't enjoy any of it.

It took me until I was in my late thirties before I realised that I was asexual. Even then it took me a bit longer to embrace the identity.

As an autistic person, being asexual is a bit fraught, as the stereotype around sexuality and autism is that we are all asexual, and that if we like sex, we must be heterosexual. This of course is nonsense. Autistic people are often interested in sex and are often gay, lesbian, pansexual, bi+, polyamorous, or any number of other sexualities. I don't like fitting a stereotype, but I can't help it! I suppose I am not responsible for the stereotype, but it still bothers me. This view is also prevalent in the broader disability community and particularly in the intellectual disability space.

Another issue around asexuality is people thinking I must be a prude. I am actually a long way from being a prude. In fact, I am very sex positive. I think if people are enjoying sex, and they are consenting adults, then by all means let them go for it! Sexual activity between consenting adults is absolutely OK and enjoyable – or so I am told – and I reckon they should do it to their hearts' content! I am far from prudish.

I am also aromantic (or "aro") – and as an aside, my spellchecker doesn't think aromantic is a word – we evidently still have a bit of a way to go! I do not have any interest in having intimate relationships. When I was younger, I thought I had to have a relationship. That was what people did, so I thought I should do it, too, but it turns out relationships are not for me. I have not had a relationship since 2004 and that is actually just fine. In fact, it is much easier. I am not lonely or sad. I like my own company and it means I can do a load of interesting things like giving talks which make the world a better place (well, I hope they do!). I do have what I would call an aesthetic attraction to people. This is not sexual attraction, and I don't want a relationship with them. It is when I like to look at someone. My aesthetic attraction is to androgynous-looking folks and women police officers (long story…). The lovely thing about not being interested in sex or dating is that I don't need to be in a relationship in order to be happy and fulfilled. I am absolutely OK for it to be just me at Yennski HQ with my kitty and with my work and my friends. I have no issues around being single. Single is absolutely fine.

One thing that I want to clarify is the difference between asexuality and incels. Incel means involuntarily celibate. This is men who cannot find a partner and are often ideologically anti-women. This is very different to asexuals / Aces. Aces are usually comfortable with not having sexual partners, whereas incels are not. I view the attitude of incels as epitomised by the concept of "I need to get a girlfriend, as if a female partner were a possession. I have had incels on my social media in the past, and I find their approach to women very problematic and offensive. Incels are very different to Aces.

My own Ace identity properly started a few years ago. I had known I was asexual for some time but hadn't really identified with it publicly. I thought it was almost a negative thing, a negation. How could I have an identity based on something I didn't do? Eventually, I came around to seeing my Ace identity as part of what made me who I am and as being just as important as my other identities. I became a very out loud and proud Ace. I now talk about my asexuality quite a lot. I think it is good to share with the world so that other Ace people can feel proud to be themselves.

Conclusion

I want a world where everyone feels able to be "out" with their sexuality and gender – a world where gender diversity and the expression of gender in all its beautiful forms is the norm and people do not face hatred or bigotry. I see signs of this being possible, but it does require effort and advocacy – and I should add activism – in order to bring this about. It is important not to be complacent and assume everything will somehow just get better in the inclusion space. It won't. It is important to promote inclusion and challenge bigotry wherever it occurs. Gender identity and sexuality to my mind are beautiful things. Knowing your identity, being respected and accepted – everyone has the right to that.

6
Managing sensory processing issues

Addressing sensory issues

> Sensory processing is the way that a person perceives, processes and organises the information that they receive through their senses – hearing, sight, touch, smell, taste and movement. This sensory information comes from one's own body and the environment around you. (Aspect, 2017)

Sensory processing disorder (SPD) is a condition that affects how a person's brain processes sensory information. Sensory processing disorder can affect all of a person's senses, some of them, or just one. Sensory processing usually means someone is overly sensitive to stimuli that other people are not. Not all autistic people have sensory processing disorder, but many do. For example, up to 90 per cent of autistic children have sensory processing disorder (Suarez, 2018). Sensory issues can take a number of forms including issues with sound, light, smell, taste and also interoception and proprioceptive issues. Interoception is the sense of what is going on in the body, such as heat, hunger, and so on, and proprioception is the sense of where we are in space, such as the distance between us and another person or object. Sensory processing can involve negative and positive experiences, with some people being sensory seekers.

Sensory issues were not well understood in the past, but now the wider world has more knowledge of the need for sensory accessibility with things like low sensory hours at supermarkets and quiet spaces in many other commercial settings and workplaces. While this is a good thing, it could definitely be taken further. The other thing to be aware of is that it is not only autistic people who benefit from sensory interventions. Some neurotypical people also find lower sensory environments to be more pleasant, such as not having loud music in a restaurant or glaring lights.

It can be said that sensory issues are accessibility issues in a similar way to providing physical accessibility for wheelchair users. This is particularly the case with sensory accommodations in the workplace. Accommodations at work can include changing lighting from fluorescent to incandescent or removing overhead lighting and replacing it with a lamp, providing noise cancelling headphones or providing a private bathroom to avoid toilet smells. Another accommodation can be around being at work at different times to colleagues or supporting staff to work from home.

In the future, I would like to see sensory accessibility expanded and a greater focus on sensory needs across the board, not just for an hour a day!

The need for sensory accessibility and understanding (Purkis, 2020)

There are a number of conditions and experiences which autistic people often have in addition to autism. These include other neurodivergent conditions (e.g. ADHD, dyspraxia, dyslexia, Tourette's), alexithymia (or emotion blindness), prosopagnosia (or face blindness), interoception issues, and sensory processing issues. Almost every autistic person I have met has one or more of these tattributes. I call them Venn diagram conditions as they overlap with autism, but a person does not necessarily need to be autistic in order to have them. For example, I have a good friend who has sensory processing issues, but to my knowledge he is not autistic.

Sensory processing issues can be overwhelming and impact significantly on a person's ability to navigate life. I have a number of sensory issues, mostly related to smell and noise. Having construction work going on can put me into a heightened state of stress. I have anxiety issues around home maintenance, and I live in an apartment block. This means that when I hear a neighbour's water running, I have a combination of negative sensory experience and high anxiety. I sit in my home longing for the neighbours to stop running their taps. It is horrible. Smell is a big one for me too. I remember going out for breakfast with some disability advocates. My friend ordered an omelette with truffles shaved onto it at the table. I absolutely hate mushrooms of all kinds. The smell of the truffles was so awful, I had to sit at a different table until my friend finished her omelette. The smell of truffles actually gave me flashbacks for about a month, and I could almost feel the smell inside me. It was really horrible.

The thing about sensory issues is that they are unique to each person. The other thing about them is that most people do not have sensory issues and so have no way of understanding what it is like to experience them. This means when I complain that a smell is horrible, another person does not share the experience and so will often dismiss my concerns. Sensory input is how we understand the world around us. It is our reality, how we make sense of the world. But what is real for me is not real for someone else. This can make it almost impossible to communicate effectively about how awful a sensory experience might be.

Another issue with sensory processing difficulties is that quite a lot of the people who experience them are neurodivergent Moreover, autistic and other neurodivergent people are a minority and face discrimination and disadvantage. This means that if we raise an issue with a sensory thing, we might not be listened to. This kind of invalidation of neurodivergent experience is rife and happens in a number of domains. This is often heightened if the person bringing up sensory issues is a child because children are often not heard by adults, and neurodivergent children particularly so. You can no doubt imagine how upsetting and frustrating this is for the individual.

Sensory distress can be extreme and make it impossible to do things that others take for granted, like going to work, to school, or even just being at home. I have a friend who finds most electric lights overwhelmingly unpleasant. They give her migraines and make her life really, really unpleasant. She is so affected by lights that she wears a blindfold when inside and uses a white cane. To a person who doesn't understand sensory issues, this would probably seem baffling, and they may think my friend was being overly dramatic. These attitudes are really challenging when a person is trying to manage the impact of sensory issues and can just make things more difficult. Basically, if someone says something is too loud, smelly, or bright, then it is.

The workplace can be a sensory nightmare, and it can be difficult for some people to access necessary adjustments at work for sensory reasons. That being said, sensory accessibility in the workplace is the same as any other accessibility needs such as ramps and lifts for wheelchair users. Employers are required to provide accessible workplaces, and if that means sensory accessibility, then so be it. Some people are unable to work at all without sensory interventions. This means that employers may miss out on the skills and expertise a neurodivergent employee might offer if given the right supports around sensory issues, and more to the point, neurodivergent people might be excluded from employment.

There needs to be a lot of education around sensory issues. Sensory issues can keep people away from doing things that they enjoy and are good at. And it isn't usually all that difficult to provide an accessible environment. I have a friend who wears a baseball cap to her job as a university lecturer to avoid glary lights in the lecture theatre. I use the accessible bathroom at my work – partially due to gender reasons but also due to toilet smells being a major sensory issue for me. Society needs to become more sensory aware. I think that would be really helpful for so many people, and it would be nice not to have to launch into a detailed explanation of sensory issues and instead just say, "it's too noisy" without needing to elaborate.

"How can you not hear that?" Communicating sensory difficulties (Purkis, 2016)

I'm not sure if this is the case for anyone else, but the older I get, the worse my sensory sensitivities are. I used to be able to eat almost anything and it all tasted good and had a texture which didn't revolt me. Now I am anxious about going to restaurants in case they have nothing I can happily eat. I eat exactly the same dish every night unless I get takeaway, in which case I usually order the same dish! (Except for pizza. I think it's pretty hard to make pizza horrible.) To the horror of my vegetarian, vegan, and health-conscious friends, the things I am able to eat mostly come from the meat group or the sugar group! I am only 42, so I worry that if I get old, I might only have one thing I can eat!

I also have an increasingly heightened sense of smell. I have always had an acute sense of smell, but it is getting ridiculous. The MC at the event I spoke at yesterday was running around all day and was evidently concerned he might be a bit stinky. I watched in horror as he liberally squirted himself with some foul deodorant thing. It permeated the room for hours! And public toilets are possibly my least favourite place at the moment. I work in a big office building, and going to the bathroom can be a disturbing and overwhelming experience. It's not that my colleagues are gross. They aren't at all – it's that my sense of smell is incredibly sensitive, so any unpleasant smell is magnified beyond normal levels.

And the one I have not experienced much before but which I find I gets quoted a lot these days is a variety of auditory sensitivities. The sounds of construction work are the worst. That noise results in an almost murderous rage. I have to be somewhere else if construction is going on. I also hate water sounds indoors and any unidentified mechanical humming sounds. Sometimes I can feel a building trembling in time to some machinery sound. It's horrible.

I'm pretty certain my autistic readers will all be reading this and thinking, "yup, sensory stuff is nasty", although their sensitivities may be different to mine. Most autistic people seem to have heightened senses. For some, these can be pleasant, but for many, they are negative and can be highly upsetting.

I think one of the worst things about sensory issues is the lack of understanding that the wider world has about them. For me, some sensory experiences are completely overwhelming and either cause furious anger or severe anxiety. When they are happening, I find it almost impossible to concentrate on the things going on at the same time. If I am at work in a meeting and there are construction sounds nearby, I am not very attentive to the discussion in the meeting. It probably looks like I am not paying attention. I don't think anyone else is thinking about the background noise. They may not even be aware of it, but for me, it is boring into my brain and making me want yell and swear and run away, yet none of those things are appropriate in the workplace. Of course, I have a very supportive and lovely employer, so if sensory issues were impacting my performance at work, I would feel very happy to tell my manager, who would consult with me about the issue and we would work together to resolve it, But not everyone has that kind of workplace and some people are "suffering in silence", so to speak.

Imagine if you are a person who has not disclosed their autism with their manager and a significant sensory issue comes up. You have to do something about it, so you try to explain to your manager what the issue is. They have no frame of reference for what you are saying. It is a situation which is completely outside of their experience. This usually means that the other person – no matter how kind or supportive they are – has very little way to understand your experience and empathise with you. They might ask something like "You can hear the fluorescent lights buzzing? Have you been smoking weed or something?" That lack of understanding tends to lead to a lack of taking your concern seriously.

Another issue involves explaining your need for sensory changes to people who are themselves the cause of the sensory issues – the neighbour who plays music with booming bass which drives you to distraction, for example. Addressing these issues requires skills around assertiveness and boundary setting, which can be difficult for autistic folks. Sensory issues with neighbours can be horrific. People have sold their houses over this sort of issue. In fact, raising noise or other issues with neighbours can also result in conflict and blame, which can compound one issue with another.

Remember that your experience is correct. Just because other people haven't experienced it does not invalidate it. Articulating what the issue is and thinking of some strategies to address it can be useful. For me, I often play music or the television when I am at home and there are noises which upset me. If it is overwhelming and this is feasible, I will leave the house. The toilet situation at work is beyond my powers to fix – you can't really ask people to stop going to the toilet! I tell myself I have to go there and that I will only be in the cubicle for a little while, which doesn't address the experience but which helps me to cope better. With food sensitivities, I look online at the menu of a restaurant I am going to the day before and research any ingredients or processes I haven't come across before. Then I know what to order and am much less anxious, but this stuff is really difficult. I would like to see more information for non-autistic people about sensory issues and what they mean to people experiencing them.

Sensory issues are accessibility issues (Purkis, 2019)

Last year, I went to a breakfast with some of the disability community leadership people in Canberra. It was at a nice café, and two of the people at the table ordered an omelette with black truffles. The server came over and shaved truffles generously on both the omelettes. I struggle with eating mushrooms and fungus and had never been in close proximity to truffles before. The smell emanating from the offending luxury breakfast was so overpowering, I had to sit at another table some distance from everyone else. I imagine they may have thought I was quite strange, but I really needed to be away from that smell.

That is a fairly clear example of sensory processing disorder (SPD), something which many people – and a great many autistic people – experience. I might point out that you do not need to be autistic to have SPD and that you do not need to have SPD to be autistic. However, there is a big overlap, despite SPD not being the exclusive domain of autistic people.

Sensory issues are serious. People have quit perfectly good jobs or sold their home to escape a sensory issue. One of the problems with sensory processing issues is that people believe their senses are reality, their "truth". The way you interpret the world is through things like sight, smell, and sound. You cannot experience another person's senses. Unless you have reason to think otherwise, your senses are the "truth". So, when somebody needs to move to another table at a restaurant because of the smell of your delicious breakfast, it can seem odd. If an employee tells their manager that they cannot work in LED lighting and could they please have an alternative form of lighting for their desk, the manager might dismiss the concern because it is not their own reality.

Sensory issues can impact on a range of experiences. Sensory processing issues can contribute to overload and "meltdown". They can mean people avoid a situation, such as kids going to school. Some people are unable to articulate their sensory distress, which can make it almost impossible to address the issue. This can relate to interoception (the sense of what is happening within the body). Emma Goodall's excellent *Interoception 101* resource includes strategies for building interoception which can help people be aware of when sensory things are overwhelming, if they are not already able to do that.

Sensory issues can be dismissed by people who "don't get it". This can be immensely frustrating and result in anxiety and feelings of disempowerment. Imagine if you spent a month plucking up the courage to raise a concern with your manager at work and they simply dismissed your concern and said, "those lights aren't bright" and then didn't address the issue.

Sometimes having sensory sensitivity can be dangerous and result in some very negative outcomes. An example of this is a person with SPD who is in a locked psychiatric ward. There is no escape from whatever sensory nasty is happening, and they are likely to feel particularly trapped, stressed, and much more prone to overload and meltdown. They may react with aggression simply because they are so overwhelmed and feel that nothing can help them. This is particularly the case if they have raised their concern with hospital staff and nothing was done. This situation can result in some terrible outcomes and illustrates how important it is to take sensory sensitivities seriously.

Some key points about sensory processing include the following:
- Everyone has different sensory experiences; there is no one experience; and things which don't seem loud or smelly to others can be overwhelming.
- Even "pleasant" sensory things like perfume and music can be unpleasant and overwhelming for some people.

- If someone raises a concern around a sensory issue, take notice of it and act.
- Sensory issues can contribute to how someone acts. If a person is overloaded, then they are more likely to demonstrate "difficult" behaviour.
- People in all areas of society need to understand sensory issues and their impact, especially managers, teachers, and health workers.

Conclusion

Sensory issues are accessibility issues. As everyone has the right to have accessibility for physical access, so too everyone deserves the right to not be subjected to a sensory onslaught when using facilities.

While things have improved in recent years, it is important to ensure that they continue to do so and that business owners and employers provide the required supports and interventions to accommodate people's sensory needs.

Lastly, I would like to see the gains advocates and activists have made in this area be consolidated and expanded upon so that people's sensory needs can be accommodated.

7
Mental health – places within the mind

Managing anxiety

Problematic anxiety is common among autistic people. Uncertainty and inconsistencies are things autistic people experience which often result in high anxiety. Just navigating life in a mostly neurotypical world can result in anxiety. Many autistic people have anxiety disorders, which include phobias, generalised anxiety disorder, obsessive compulsive disorder, panic disorder, and post-traumatic stress disorder (National Autistic Society, 2024).

Managing anxiety – thoughts and strategies (Purkis, 2023)

I am pretty much constantly anxious. I worry about everything from concerns that my emails aren't sending to stressing about home maintenance. Anxiety is definitely not my friend as for me, extreme anxiety can turn into psychosis, which usually results in my taking years to recover and having to take months off work and spend a lot of time in hospital. I have attempted suicide before due to high anxiety. I actually tried to take my life because my internet didn't work a couple of years ago. Because of this, I get anxious about being anxious!

I want to share some of the things I do to address anxiety – they aren't always 100 per cent effective, but they do help me. The first is simple: medication. I went through most of my life not having any medication for my anxiety. The problem was that whenever I was in hospital and under the care of a psychiatrist, I was psychotic. Psychosis trumps pretty much everything in mental health care. If you are psychotic, it is also quite hard to express or articulate what is going on. Because of this, I never managed to tell any hospital psychiatrists who were responsible for changing my medication that anxiety was destroying me! Then in 2021, I was in hospital and I was not psychotic. I explained to the doctor that my anxiety about the internet not working had resulted in a suicide attempt. He said, "I will address your anxiety" and instantly put me on medication for anxiety, which completely changed my life! I still get anxious but nowhere near as badly, and since then I have had no psychotic episodes.

Another strategy is around thinking. A mental health worker once told me that if thoughts were making me anxious, I should imagine that they were a person knocking on the door. I couldn't help them being there, but I could decide whether or not to let them in. I took this one step further and imagined that Donald Trump was at the door…and there is no way in the world I would ever let him into my house! I now just think "Eep! Trump's at the door!" This works quite nicely.

I also practice my own kind of mindfulness by watching relaxing scenery on YouTube. This works well – and my cat enjoys it too!

I don't like when people say, "oh, don't worry about that". If anxiety listened to logic, then psychologists would all be unemployed! Problematic anxiety is by its nature illogical. If I could just tell myself not to worry, then life would be a lot easier and I would have spent a lot less of my time in hospital!

I do some deep breathing when I am really anxious. This helps. Anxiety for me is a very physical thing. I feel tight in my chest and belly, and my heart races. So deep breathing is a physical means of addressing anxiety and helps me slow down.

I also often tell a friend if I am anxious about something as they can put it into perspective. I DON'T need to die because my internet isn't working!

Distraction is a big plus as well. This involves doing something enjoyable to occupy your brain. It works by taking your mind off the anxiety. Distraction is my go-to mental health strategy, and many other people find it helpful too.

I see a psychologist, which helps. A good psychologist can make a big difference. It can take a while to find a good psychologist but a good one is a blessing. Finding one who understands autism and neurodivergence is really important. You can ask around your neurodivergent network to see who is good, although you should be aware that different people may experience the same psychologist differently.

Anxiety is not my friend. While it is a natural function passed down from our ancient ancestry, for me it is more harmful than useful. I am much less anxious than I was, but it is still an issue. Strategies are really helpful and you can build your knowledge of what works over time.

Accessing support and other strategies

Accessing supports for mental health for autistic people can be very difficult. We can face discrimination or poor treatment from clinicians who have little or no idea about how to effectively support autistic people. Things are gradually changing in this space, but it is still a significant issue. Some autistic people find mental health services so unhelpful that they simply don't access support. Mental health services can be actively unhelpful. I always liken it to calling the plumber and they come in with the best goodwill in the world, but they break your toilet!

The next two posts relate to accessing mental health services – something autistic people can struggle with and find difficult to navigate. There is a need for a lot of work in this space, including around educating mental health clinicians and addressing the discrimination and ableism around mental health issues in society. My posts to follow will respectively delve into the interesting topics of imposter syndrome and associated anxiety as well as the mental health benefits of pet ownership.

What happens when mental health services get it right? (Purkis, 2020)

I was in one or another psychiatric ward since mid-October l2019 to August 2021 . I was prescribed ADHD medication which interacted with my illness and made me psychotic. The way my illness usually works is that I get really anxious, become psychotic, become depressed and/or manic, became suicidal, and then end up somewhere on the other side and ready to get back into things. The ADHD meds, as far as I can tell, tripped off the psychosis and almost six months of misery has ensued.

Usually when I talk about mental health and autism, I tease out all the negatives in treatment – nurses who are uncaring, processes which are not autism-friendly, sensory nightmares in hospital settings, that kind of thing. While these were the case in two of the hospitals I stayed in recently – and in fact in pretty much every inpatient setting I have ever been in – they are not the case in my current residence. I want to unpack some of the positives about where I am with the hope of setting an example for good practice. What are they doing right here and why is it helpful?

I am staying at a rehabilitation hospital attached to the University of Canberra. It has been open for just over a year and exists to rehabilitate people with complex mental health issues. On my first day, I received loads of knocks on the door from different workers. I soon worked out that my treating team involves a consultant psychiatrist, a psychologist, a neuropsychologist, an occupational therapist, a social worker, an exercise physiologist, two peer workers, a dietitian, and two allied health assistants. There are also nurses, most of whom are lovely and very helpful. The cleaning staff are lovely and know me by name. Everything about the hospital is set up to facilitate rehabilitation. It is a true multidisciplinary team.

The doctors here are unusual in that they listen and change their tactics based on feedback from patients. My doctor is extremely available, not minding when I knock on her door. She listens to my experience, and any medication changes are done in conjunction and consultation with me.

The response from the hospital to the Covid-19 pandemic has been clearly articulated and regularly discussed. Doctors have asked people to come to them with concerns. There does not seem to be any panic about Covid-19 among staff or patients. There are hand sanitisers everywhere, and the morning meeting involves being reminded to stay 1.5m apart, but it is all pretty matter-of-fact. In the morning meeting, one of the peer workers usually gets everyone to say something we are happy about.

Unlike many wards, patient complaints about their physical health or things like sensory issues are listened to – well, in my experience at least. The level of disempowerment when someone ignores these needs is immense, and it is such a relief when staff actually listen to you.

There is a sensory room here, and people are encouraged to use it. I love the sensory room and often go there when I am distressed. Unlike many wards where patients are given chemical restraint (i.e. medication is seen as the solution to everything), here extra medication is given after other avenues (such as the sensory room) are exhausted.

Nurses usually have time to talk to you if you are having a tough time. This is a really important one for me as I often need to talk to someone when I am unwell. Another notable difference is that if you knock on the nurse's station window, someone will come and talk to you right away. There is one ward in Canberra where this definitely isn't the case!

I think the attitudes here come from the premise that we are all people – all equal. The idea is that anyone can become unwell. As an autistic person, I find the ethos of this hospital very positive. It evidently isn't impossible to make the necessary changes either as they have been made in this setting, so presumably other hospitals could follow suit. I don't see a lot of specific autism knowledge here, but I see something possibly equally positive – staff treating people with respect and dignity. I am trying to boost the autism knowledge, of course, but that focus on respect and inclusion is a great basis for this place. If all mental health facilities had a similar level of respect and dignity, then inpatient services would be less unpleasant and would probably actually help people.

Addressing self-doubt and impostor syndrome

Stop, impostor! Impostor syndrome – confidence and intersectionality (Purkis, 2021)

I will preface this by saying that the introduction to this post is not intended to brag but to illustrate a problem I have – that of impostor syndrome.

I am the author of nine published books: an autobiography, a book on employment for autistic young people, one on mental health, two on resilience, one for autistic kids on self-empowerment, one for autistic women on navigating life well, a book of my poems. and a book for trans and gender-divergent autistic adults. I have chapters or poems in a further ten publications, and have two books in production and one under contract. These books are but one example of the impressive things I do, but how do you imagine I view this? Basically, I mostly dismiss and devalue every achievement I have and feel like I am a big fraud with nothing to offer the world.

The interesting thing about this is that I am far from alone. Many people also experience impostor syndrome. Another interesting thing is that mostly – in my experience – the people experiencing impostor syndrome are those who belong to at least one intersectional group. I have a few "diversity" boxes that I tick – I am autistic and ADHD; I have schizophrenia; and I am non-binary and asexual. I spent many years in my early adulthood in poverty and some years in prison. Even though my socio-economic status is now at the higher end of the scale, 15 years of poverty have taken their toll on my feelings about myself and my place in the world. Likewise, I have not been in trouble with the law since 1999, but the time I spent in the criminal justice system took its toll on my confidence and sense of identity.

When it comes to impostor syndrome, intersectionality is often – although not always – a big factor. For me, I experience impostor syndrome on a few fronts. It makes me question my worth and my contribution to the world. I worry that my books are meaningless and that I actually have no expertise on anything I have written about and am a complete fraud. I doubt my credentials and worry that I am just an opinionated person who has nothing useful to say about anything, and that the people who buy my books are wasting their money. This is not just a fleeting thought or doubt; rather, it is a deeply help belief. Even writing about it now adds fuel to the fire of impostor syndrome and I worry I am putting things into the world which are negative and unhelpful.

The other element of my own impostor syndrome is all about my identity. I worry that I am "not transgender enough" or that people will question my autism, ADHD, and schizophrenia diagnoses. Whenever someone misgenders me or makes a comment about my sense of style being feminine, I get anxious and worry that I am a fraud as a non-binary and transgender person. When I first came out as non-binary, this was a big problem and I worried about it all the time. Thankfully, I came to the realisation that anyone who identifies as transgender is in fact transgender. It is an identity and you own it yourself. And looking at my past, it is absolutely obvious that I am – and have always been – transgender and non-binary! Logic tells me that there is no doubt about that fact – although, of course, anxiety and logic don't go hand in hand and impostor syndrome is related to anxiety.

Like other kinds of anxiety, impostor syndrome doesn't listen to logic. I am one of the most accomplished people I know, but that makes zero difference as far as how I view myself. Impostor syndrome can be fed by negative messaging and assumptions of incompetence from other people in relation to a person being Disabled. Disabled people are often treated like any minor thing we do is an "inspiration" – something which feeds directly into impostor syndrome and a lack of confidence. We also often get messaging that we are incapable of doing anything useful or doing things that others can do – something which can result in a lack of confidence and in impostor syndrome.

I think that building self-confidence can be challenging, but it is a good way of helping to address impostor syndrome. However, there is a thing which is like impostor syndrome but is sort of its opposite. That is where a person is wrongly overconfident. Similarly to impostor syndrome, this thing relates to intersectionality, but rather than resulting from someone feeling devalued as a member of intersectional groups, it tends to happen to people from positions of privilege. An example is a colleague I had many years ago. He was a white cis gender heterosexual middle-class man. He applied for a promotion to two levels above his substantive work classification. I remember this because I applied for a promotion (for one level of advancement) at the same time and was convinced I wouldn't get it. My level of confidence as an employee was quite low and I only applied for the promotion because my manager recommended it. This fellow applied for a position which was way beyond his capability because he genuinely believed he could do it. He ended up leaving the workplace about three months after he got the promotion because he was not capable of fulfilling the role and kept making mistakes.

Of course, people from privileged groups can get impostor syndrome, and it is more complex than "diversity good, privileged bad". But I do think there is a strong connection between intersectionality, identity, and confidence, and impostor syndrome (and overconfidence too!). It would be nice if the people who lacked confidence could be encouraged to have a more realistic view of their capabilities – both for them but also so that they would be more likely to share their skills and talents and thoughts with the world.

The value of pets

Pets and assistance animals can play a big part in promoting good mental health and addressing anxiety and depression for autistic people. Many autistic people are strongly bonded with their pets and assistance animals – be they cats, dogs, rats, birds, snakes, or any other kind of animal. The bond with animals can be immense, and many autistic people are more closely bonded with their animals than with the human inhabitants of their world.

Little kitty therapists (Purkis, 2023)

I recently became human parent to a little tortoiseshell kitty who I have named Sunflower. She is absolutely beautiful and the latest in a long line of feline friends that I have been privileged to share my home and life with.

I always say that I am better with a cat and I am. I have loved cats from the moment I discovered their existence. They are very good for my mental health. In fact, I can credit a previous Yennski cat, the prince among felines that was Mr Kitty, with keeping me out of the psych ward for many years. I remember shortly after I adopted him that a mental health worker said there was a spot in a respite service that I had used in the past. I replied that I didn't need it because I was in respite every single day without leaving the house due to my new kitty.

I used to call Mr Kitty my "little black kitty therapist". They are actually ALL therapists. Sunflower makes me so happy. Before I adopted her, I had stress-related eczema on my hands. It was so bad that it was cracked and bleeding, but within a week of my having Sunflower, it had vanished. When I am at work, I get to the end of the day and look forward to coming home to a smoochy kitty person.

I really do go much better if I have a cat. I know cats on a deep level. I can't do human body language, but feline body language is easy! Patting a purring cat is better for my mental health than almost anything else. The pet rescue service that I adopted Sunflower from was extremely strict. I had to satisfy a lot of criteria – which, of course, I am all for! I wouldn't want an abuser adopting kitties. In response to my application, they said that any cat would be very happy to have me as their human. I really do love cats and I connect with them more than I do with most humans. I have said in the past that if when I die I go to wherever the cats go, I will be very happy! I used to say that I could pat Mr Kitty for a happy eternity, and the same is true for Sunflower.

I am actually not alone among autistic people here. A large number of autistic people connect on a significant level with animals – be they pets, or with nature generally. My mum is autistic. She doesn't bond with cats or dogs but is very much a fan of nature and all its beauty. She knows the Latin names of thousands of plants and is something of an expert on fungi. I do know a lot of autistic people who have a similar bond to cats as I do, or some with dogs or birds or snakes. Our animal friends and companions "get" us more neurotypical people do. I never have to worry about Sunflower bullying, abusing, ghosting, or ostracising me. I understand her and I think she understands me in her sweet little furry way. There is no confusing complexity in our relationship. She is easy for me to connect with. She will never gaslight me or manipulate me. I am not sure why other autistic people are so often close to animals and nature, but we definitely seem to be. Maybe it is for similar reasons to me, maybe not.

Conclusion

Mental health is a big topic, and autistic people often struggle with mental health issues and also with accessing services if past experiences with services may have been negative. While things are gradually changing in the mental health treatment space, there is still a way to go before we can say it is inclusive for autistic people accessing help. A better world would see mental health clinicians understanding and respecting autistic people, listening and learning from the experience of their autistic patients. A better world would also see significantly more autistic clinicians, and particularly doctors and psychiatrists. There has been a significant shift in autism and mental health knowledge over the past 20–30 years. This is evidenced through the neurodiversity movement and changes in the provision of mental health services, and demonstrates that things can change for the better in this area. It is important for advocates to keep raising issues where they exist and working to promote positive change in the area of providing inclusive and helpful mental health care for autistic people.

8
Employment and the workplace

Employment can pose a significant challenge for autistic people. Unemployment and underemployment rates are high and recruitment processes are often exclusionary – even if not intentionally (Amaze, 2023). Things like CVs and job interviews do not generally enable autistic applicants to shine, and workplaces can be unsupportive, meaning that many autistic people churn through unsuitable jobs despite having skills and experience which many employers seek out.

Navigating employment can be a nightmare for autistic people. Attitudes around autism and employment remain very negative, with many employers not wanting to hire them and workplaces not being autism-friendly (Griffiths, 2020). Recently, things have started to change, but there is still a long way to go. Traditionally, attitudes around autism – and disability generally – and employment centre on the perceived deficits and difficulties rather than the skills. Immensely talented autistic people who present and communicate differently to their neurotypical peers face discrimination and the assumption that they can't work – or shouldn't work. The reality is that while some autistic people genuinely cannot work, others can and do – and often do an excellent job.

It doesn't take too long to figure out an autistic person's significant skills – the attributes which might have put off employers can actually mean the person is a great fit for the job! There is a right to work and that extends to autistic people too.

New adventures – doing things you love (Purkis, 2024)

Yesterday, I left my job after 17 years. This was A Big Deal and the result of a variety of things. Despite wandering around the house the day that I gave my notice saying to myself, "ha ha, you're unemployed!!" I do have some sources of income. I am now – after 17 years – basically a professional autistic, ADHD, non-binary, and asexual advocate. I will be doing consultancy, coaching, writing, and presenting as a job. My income will be derived from doing something I love. How absolutely wonderful. I am very excited – and a little anxious from time to time. I will wake up on Monday and not go to work. Wow! (Well, given how impractical and confused I can be, I will probably wake up on Monday and get dressed for work, walk out the door, and remember just as I am getting on the tram!!)

I have five employers lined up, so imagine I may actually get more work than I can manage! However, I have essentially been doing two full-time jobs for almost 20 years, so I think I should be OK.

My new life adventure gets me thinking about other people's employment journeys. The wonderful Barb Cook and I wrote a book called *Planning Your Career through Intense Interests* (Purkis and Cook, 2023) a couple of years ago. It is aimed at autistic young people and looks at using your passion to drive a career.

The ability to pursue your passionate interests as your job is a lovely thing indeed. Goal-setting and career-planning strategies can help identify what skills and interests you have.

I wish everyone career success and the ability to use their paid work to pursue their passions. I am excited at my own career adventure. A job should be enjoyable and engaging. It should help people build their knowledge, skills, and wisdom. It should support development and engagement and self-esteem . People – including autistic people – should have the opportunity for career advancement if they want it and are capable. There is a pervasive view among some managers that they have done an autistic employee a favour by employing them and they should stay at entry level and be grateful for it. This simply isn't true. As a public servant, I was promoted twice in my career because I was capable of working at a higher level. Work should be inclusive and free from bigotry and hate and bullying. Being in the workplace should provide a sense of being part of something bigger, of making the world a better place as well as the more practical things like providing an income.

Autistic people can have a range of challenges in the workplace – often due to a lack of understanding from managers and colleagues. I had a boss once who when I raised my concerns about her ability to manage me as an autistic person said, "Oh, I know all about it. I managed an autistic person once". These sorts of attitudes are sadly quite common. However, the workplace does not need to be an unpleasant place for autistic folks. We tend to have some impressive skills which set us apart from our allistic and neurotypical peers. I have worked in areas where I was highly prized due to some of the attributes which were related to my autism.

I have been talking about autism and employment and the benefits of neurodivergent staff to employers for over ten years, and it is a great thing to open their minds to the significant benefits of employing autistic staff. In fact, one of the things I will be doing in my new career is working with employers to support them to employ neurodivergent staff. Lovely!

People should want to be at work and should ideally look forward to going to work. Of course, this often isn't the case, but it can happen, and should be supported . Some of the best jobs I have had, have been wonderful not due to the work itself but due to the managers. I once had a neurodivergent manager who was amazing. I had another manager who I loved dearly and am still in touch with after she retired many years ago. A good manager – or a bad one – can make all the difference at work.

I am happy to have had a 17-year career in the public service and I look forward to what the future may bring. When I was 25 – half my age now – I changed my life dramatically. Now I am doing it again. Scary and exciting. We will see how things go.

Oh, and as I am no longer a public servant, I can say this … I have politics! I vote Green! I really do and I always have. And I have an immense dislike of Pauline Hanson and Donald Trump and hope they both go to jail for a long, long time. Also, I think the world needs to fundamentally adjust its approach, or we will all suffer major effects of climate change!! Ah, that felt good after 17 years!

To disclose or not disclose (Purkis, 2022)

I am out loud and proud as autistic, ADHD, non-binary and asexual pretty much everywhere including at work. It does not occur to me that disclosure / coming out is an option for me! When I started my public service career, I had to provide a letter from my psychiatrist at the time about my schizophrenia, so HR knew all about that and I disclosed my autism as well. Back then, disclosure of my autism was mostly due to the fact I had published a book all about being autistic, so figured should any HR practitioners google me, they would find out anyway.

I have had almost 100 per cent positive and supportive responses to my disclosing. I do it now for similar reasons but also because I do not like to keep such important parts of my identity a secret. I also don't think it should be a secret. It is not shameful or something I want to hide.

In terms of my Queer identities, I am also open about those too for similar reasons. I always say that I don't like closets – they are dark and scary and isolating. And I don't think I should have to be in the closet about my gender and sexuality. Once again, they are not things to be ashamed of. They are actually things to be celebrated in my opinion. My being "out" also gives others license to be out themselves, which has to be a good thing.

However, not everyone has received the positive response that I have. Disclosure of neurodivergence can result in a range of unpleasant issues, ranging from not getting jobs to being passed over for career advancement to outright prejudice, and being out as a transgender or asexual person can result in a lot of bigotry and discrimination.

Disclosure and coming out are not decisions to take lightly. There can be some great consequences and some dreadful ones. I always suggest making a strategy around disclosure. Do you intend to disclose? What do you want to say? At what point in the recruitment process do you want to say it (e.g. on application, at interview, when you get offered the job, when you start or a while after you start)? Who do you want to tell (your manager, HR, your colleagues or all of these individuals)? You might not always do what you plan, but I find it helpful to have some guidance behind me before I actually do the disclosing. Also, each workplace is different, and within workplaces each team and manager are different, so what works well in one setting may not work in another.

Disclosure is a difficult topic. There is no absolutely right or absolutely wrong answer. It is a decision requiring consideration. Also, it can help to plan a contingency if disclosure goes awry. What will you do? Who will support you? Is the exclusionary behaviour against your employer's code of conduct and, if so, will you take action? The worst outcome is that you are discriminated against and lose your job. Of course, it is illegal to discriminate or terminate a person's employment due to their neurotype, sexuality or gender, but it can be very difficult to prove that is what happened.

It would be so nice if we lived in a world where we didn't even have to consider issues with disclosure and coming out, but sadly, we do not live in such a world – yet. I will continue to be out loud and proud. I remember a colleague many years ago coming up to me in the corridor and whispering, "I have schizophrenia too, but don't tell anyone". This made me so sad. I have never kept my illness a secret, but I completely understand why someone would, because there is a lot of bigotry and ableism around the diagnosis.

I sometimes think I occupy a different world to others. Over decades of employment, I have rarely encountered issues due to disclosing my autism and mental health issues or even my gender, but I know others certainly do. I don't know why I have largely escaped issues, but I have and for that I am most grateful. I want a world where disclosure isn't even a consideration – people just do it in the same way they provide an employer with other information such as their name, address or date of birth.

"W" is for "Work" (Purkis, 2022)

I wrote a book called *The Wonderful World of Work*. It is my second book and is an instructional activity-type thing for autistic teens to help prepare them for a career. On the morning that it was published, the publisher posted about it on their Facebook page. The first comment on my lovely new book was this: "The world of work for autistic people is horrible, not wonderful. I won't be buying this book!" I was of course quite horrified by this reaction. I mean, they had a point! Maybe I shouldn't have written a positive book about autism and employment? Thankfully, future reviews and commentaries on my second contribution to the literature on autism were much more positive, but it got me thinking.

I couldn't work for many years. I was simply too anxious and too much of a perfectionist. And earlier in my life I was in prison and psychiatric wards pretty much non-stop for five years, so paid employment was a fair way away from my mind. By the time I worked out that I wanted to change my ways, I realised that work was a very important thing. I was desperate to work, but it took many years to get to a place where I could work. I did what I would now call controlled challenges in order to build my confidence to work. I started by volunteering at a gallery. I really enjoyed this, and it wasn't too stressful because I wasn't getting paid (at this point in my journey I worried about being in paid work and costing the employer lots of money or making mistakes). After my volunteer job, I started a small business editing videos for my art school colleagues. And then I got a job talking about autism to schoolkids, which I loved – yes, I have always loved public speaking! I wrote a book in 2005 and it was published. This gave me enormous amounts of confidence and within three months of it being published, I applied for public service graduate roles.

Applying for the public service was a big deal. I was fairly certain I would be refused due to my schizophrenia and my extensive police history from the 1990s, but I figured that if I didn't apply but would have won a position, I would have missed out big time. However, if I applied and was unsuccessful, I would have lost nothing. "Give it a burl", thought 31-year-old Yennski, and so I did, and I was successful.

I am still in the public service 16 years later. (Note: since this post was published, I have left the public service.) It was one of the best decisions I have ever made. I had to answer a LOT of questions about my past, but I got the job and have now been promoted twice and worked in a range of really interesting and rewarding areas. My job has funded the purchase of two properties, and I am financially independent and doing meaningful and rewarding work. I absolutely love my job.

But what about the words of my reviewer and the world of work not being wonderful for autistic people? Well, they still have a point as for many autistic and neurodivergent people work is stressful and even traumatising. I have also had some of those kinds of jobs in the past.

It is quite common these days to get people listing all the positive attributes of autistic employees – attention to detail, pattern thinking, focus, passion, loyalty, that sort of thing. I wish we didn't need to do that because we lived in a world where employers were aware of the skills and gifts we bring to our jobs. There is still a way to go in that area, but things have improved in the 31 years since I first joined the workforce. Employers need more understanding and knowledge of autism. I think it is definitely changing, but it is still the case for many autistic people that their world of work is not wonderful. We also have very high rates of unemployment, underemployment and of being in unsuitable work. I want to live in a world where the world of work for neurodivergent folks is a lot more likely than not to be wonderful!

Conclusion

Things are changing in the world of autism and employment. There are now many organisations devoted to neurodivergence at work, and there is a growing view among employers that autistic and neurodivergent staff can provide a competitive advantage for their businesses. Businesses like Specialisterne and the DXC Dandelion programme, which exist in order to place autistic people in employment, have been working in this area since the mid-2010s.

However, there are still many issues facing neurodivergent and autistic employees and those seeking work. The employment rate for autistic people remains very low. The unemployment rate for autistic people is 34.1 per cent, more than three times the rate for people with disability (10.3 per cent), and almost eight times the rate of people without disability (4.6 per cent) (Australian Bureau of Statistics, 2023). More than half of unemployed autistic Australian adults (54 per cent) have never held a paid job (Amaze, 2023).

Change still needs to happen in this space and to be ongoing. Autistic people have a huge number of positive attributes to share in the workplace. The low employment rates for autistic people do not necessarily relate to their lack of skill or capability. They are more related to structural barriers, biases and assumptions among employers and to workplaces not being accessible or supportive. All these things can change, and the work which has begun recently through advocacy, activism, allyship, policymaking and inclusive service provision is a good sign. Let us hope it continues.

9
Navigating accommodation

For autistic folks, finding and keeping accommodation can be a significant challenge. Many autistic people are unemployed and receive income support, making owning – and even renting – impossible. Shared accommodation can result in inappropriate situations and difficult and strained relationships with housemates. Some autistic folks find themselves homeless – either couch-surfing, living in crisis accommodation or sleeping in their cars or on the street. Some people find themselves homeless after living in an abusive relationship. While all these issues happen for neurotypical people, they are of particular concern for autistic folks due to the vulnerabilities associated with autism and the fact that autistic people are at greater risk of violence and abuse (Gibbs and Pellicano, 2023). This is obviously something which needs to change in a big way.

When people talk about autism, they rarely talk about accommodation, but it is a significant issue for many of us. Some people live in supported accommodation, but many of us live independently – or as close to independently as possible. Accommodation – and difficulties obtaining suitable accommodation – can result in high levels of anxiety for autistic people

(Scheeren, 2021). Autism can compound issues in housing which others may not notice, such as sensory issues. So, a housing organisation or support worker may think a house or apartment is ideal, but the autistic tenant can't live there due to noises or smells or the ableist attitudes of neighbours or any number of other issues that autistic people experience but which others may be unaware of.

The blog posts in this chapter cover similar topics but from different perspectives.

Home at last (Purkis, 2020)

This post is a more personal, reflective one than usual and it is about the idea of home and how I have finally found somewhere I feel safe and happy after many years of unstable, unsuitable and stressful housing.

I moved into my new apartment on Tuesday. It is a rental, and it is the nicest place I have ever lived. It is a one-bedroom apartment, but it is huge, and I am the first occupant ever as it is brand new. I am extremely grateful for this lovely home and feel like I am living in a beautiful dream. It doesn't seem real. I have a television and DVD player in my bedroom, brand-new appliances and a great balcony. I am so happy here, I can hardly believe my luck. And I am not stressed. This is A Big Deal as the last two properties I lived in caused no end of stress and poor mental health. More about that later, but for now let's go back in time to the 1990s.

I moved out of home when I was 17. I had finished school and had a lot of issues with living at the family home. I was a socialist – a passionate interest in left-wing politics having pushed me into the embrace of the International Socialist Organisation at the age of 15. My politics meant that I was always arguing with my dad. I moved out pretty much straight after I finished school and spent some years living in share houses with fellow socialists.

In 1994, I met someone who changed the direction of my life in a big and very negative way.

"Dave" was a criminal and I ended up in a relationship with him. I got more and more involved in his world, and by the time I realised how dangerous this was, I had got too involved and was afraid to leave him given how much of his awful plans he had confided in me. We committed crimes and both went to jail. When I was released from jail, I lived with a friend I had briefly gone to university with. This did not work out as I had taken on the persona of a criminal – a fairly significant piece of masking and one which enabled me to survive in prison but put me in a very negative position in the outside world. My share house arrangement fell through when my uni friends became anxious about my frequent drug use. I moved into a boarding house and then into a house occupied by my drug dealers. After a few months, we all got evicted and I found myself homeless.

Luckily, I had friends from a theatre company who worked with women prisoners. They found me a place in the country with a woman who ran a camp for school groups and also looked after young people who had "issues" – like me. I was there for a few months and ended up in the psychiatric hospital, receiving a diagnosis of schizophrenia. At this time, I got in touch with my parents – the first time I had spoken to them in a long time. I moved back in with my parents for a year. While my parents' house was a lot nicer and more stable than any I had lived at in recent years, it was still difficult. I felt like I was living in two worlds – the druggie/criminal and the dutiful child. I felt pulled in two directions and it was very challenging.

About a year after I moved in with my parents, I got really unwell with schizophrenia again. I was delusional and thought prison was the cure for my depression, so I committed crimes with the intent of going to jail. I spent the next three years in and out of institutions – psych wards and jails. My life was pretty hellish and unstable. In 2000, things changed. I accessed help for my mental illness and started to want a better world for myself. I decided to be "ordinary" – by which I meant having an education, a professional job, a mortgage and a suit. These aspirations probably seemed ridiculous at the time, but I stuck with them, enrolling in university just a few months after I was a released from prison.

Housing was a major problem for many years. I lived in crisis housing and in mental health residential programmes. I got a public housing flat in 2003, staying there until 2007. I had a neighbour at the public housing flat who stalked me. She was jealous of any female visitors – including being jealous of my mum– and made my life a living hell. The good thing about that was that this neighbour inadvertently pushed me towards getting a full-time job so I could rent privately. In an unlikely turn of events, I obtained a public service job in 2007 and moved out of public housing, feeling very relieved and excited that my aspirations for a better life had eventuated.

I bought my own home in 2008. This might sound wonderful, and, in a way, it was, but it was also quite fraught. I could not afford a very nice or new home, so bought a flat in a very old block. It had some significant maintenance issues, which made me very anxious. So anxious in fact that in 2010 and 2019, the anxiety around my home caused psychosis. I hated this apartment and longed to leave and I finally did so this earlier this year. I sold it and moved into a rental in the same 1970s block. While it was less stressful than living in the one I had owned, the fact that it was in the same block heightened my anxiety.

I moved in here on Tuesday and I keep finding myself walking around with a big smile on my face. My new home is just lovely, and I am not at all stressed. I feel like it is my first ever "proper" home as an adult.

A number of people have said I deserve to have a nice home after all that time, and I sort of agree. Everyone deserves to have a nice home, I think, as it makes such a difference to a person's sense of well-being, inclusion and positive mental health. I am extremely grateful for my home and look forward to my 12 months here. And I suspect I may renew the lease if I can.

My accommodation journey (Purkis, 2022)

Content warning: reference to suicide, prison

Accommodation has been on my mind of late. I am about to purchase my second property, so have been reflecting on my history of housing. I am now extremely privileged in terms of income and have a well-paid, secure job – the kind of thing that banks get excited about! Most people with the sorts of experiences and issues I have are unable to even consider purchasing property, so I am very lucky indeed. I don't want to reflect on how unusual I am here – something I could definitely elaborate on, but which probably wouldn't be very interesting! I want to look at my history of difficult housing situations.

Many autistic people are in insecure housing, and many people with schizophrenia are too. And just to clarify – schizophrenia and autism are my two main "diversity"-type groups which often come with financial disadvantage attached.

When I was younger, accommodation was a huge issue. I actually belong to a third group that has significant financial disadvantage attached and that is ex-prisoners. These days, membership of that group has little to no impact on me as that occurred between 23 and 28 years ago, but at the time there was a lot of financial trouble and associated homelessness in my life.

I moved out of home when I was 17. I shared houses, and because of my autistic take on socialising not being understood and the difficulty I had in being assertive and raising issues with housemates, I went through a lot of share house situations. Then when I was 20, I went to prison and spent the next five years in and out of institutions. I lived with my parents for a year and then descended into homelessness and incarceration. When I applied for public housing, they categorised me as the highest priority as I had lived in 40 places in the preceding few years!

I remember living in a boarding house in St Kilda in Melbourne. My best friend in the house was a sex worker and heroin user. We would vent about the other women in the house who we found annoying. I hated living in this place, but I had no control over where I lived. I was too poor to take out a private rental, so I lived in supported and crisis housing. From the boarding house I moved to a property owned by a mental health charity, the Richmond Fellowship. I stayed there for just over two years. I liked this house and made friends – and a partner – from among my housemates. From there I moved to a transitional apartment while I waited for a public housing property to be available. This apartment was amazing. It had two bedrooms and bright green carpet! I would have happily lived there forever, but it was only a stopgap before I got my public housing flat, so I didn't stay long.

I thought I had done something clever when I applied for public housing. I didn't want to live in a big complex of public housing flats. I had a friend who had got her public housing application limited to properties of three floors or fewer due to her mental health and suicide risk. I figured this was a great idea, so I added that caveat to my own housing application. I figured I would get a public housing flat in a block of private rentals. I would not have to live in the ghetto! Sadly, they found me a flat in a big complex, but the highest was three floors! Because I was on the priority list, I could not decline the offer of this place.

I hated my public housing flat from the moment I saw it. There was damp actually running down the walls. My neighbours were mostly people with alcohol and drug issues. I was still desperate to be socially accepted, so I became an alcoholic myself in order to fit in and win the approval of my neighbours. I lived in this apartment for four years. One of my neighbours was a stalker. She was awful and never left me alone. She would glare at any female visitors I had – including my mum! The threat of being robbed or bashed was quite large at this place. At this point in my life, I was going to university and planning to change my life for the better. The flat – and particularly my stalker – stood for everything I wanted to get away from. While I was staying here, I decided I needed a full-time, well-paid job. I set about making that the path I would take.

It was not easy changing my life, but it was possible. It must be possible because I did it. I got my job, moved to Canberra and life was, well, different. I bought a property in 2008. It was a bit of a compromise. The flat was very old, and I kept getting plumbing issues. These resulted in high anxiety which – on two occasions – turned into psychosis and resulted in my being extremely unwell and taking months and years as sick leave from my work.

I sold that property in 2020. The plan was for me to buy another one, but I was way too anxious at that point. It has only been in recent months that I have felt able to purchase somewhere, and to be honest, I am still not sure if it will be OK or if the process will make me unwell. I figure it is best to try such things and not be hampered by anxiety. So, I will have my Castle Yennski – or as I am tempted to call it Chateau Overachiever – very soon. I am very grateful for how all these things seem to have worked out. Had you told me in 2000, when I had just been released from prison and was living in very unpleasant boarding house accommodation, that I would have the accommodation that I do now, I would have been very surprised – and probably told you to keep off the drugs!

Conclusion

Everyone should have the ability to live in secure and appropriate housing. It is the most basic of human needs as well as being a human right. Autistic folks often miss out on access to appropriate housing – and in some cases any housing at all. Autistic folks can be particularly vulnerable in this area, and that needs to be understood and addressed.

Housing authorities and real estate agents require more understanding around the needs of their autistic tenants / clients. It would be great if more autistic people could own their own homes. In order to achieve this, lenders and real estate agents should have a good understanding of autism and neurodivergence, particularly as it relates to housing. It would also be great if people stopped making assumptions about autistic people's ability to purchase or rent property. These sorts of assumptions can actually have the perverse effect of making it more difficult for autistic folks to purchase or rent property due to the deficits thinking of those around them in relation to autism and independence. It should be noted that owning property is not for everyone and is not somehow "better" than renting, sharing or living in supported accommodation. If your house is secure, safe and provides what you need in a house (or apartment etc.), that is a great outcome regardless of whether you own, rent, share or any other arrangement.

I want to see a world where everyone has access to suitable housing, including autistic folks. Appropriate housing is a human right (Section 25 *Disability Discrimination Act*, 1992) – and definitely a human need! I think greater understanding is required and more of the funding related to supporting autistic folks to thrive needs to be directed to accommodation.

Epilogue

I hope you enjoyed my various thoughts and reflections on life, the universe (or maybe the Yenniverse?), neurodivergent and Queer identity and lots of other things! I hope you found the posts enlightening and that they increased your awareness around neurodivergent experience – and how to support and promote understanding, inclusion and respect for neurodivergent – and Queer – people.

The posts featured in this book were written between 2014 and 2024. I usually write one post each week on a different topic. There are quite a lot of different topics. I have enjoyed reading the older ones and reflecting on my last ten years as an advocate and author. When I started out with the blogs, I had two published books. Now I have 18! Since I started blogging, I have done some lovely things – giving my second TEDx talk, my mum's getting her autism diagnosis in her 60s, adopting lovely Sunflower Kitty and doing lots of writing and presentations.

I am aware I am not a very likely sort of person. A clozapine nurse I used to have called me "an anomaly", and I suspect he was right. The beautiful thing about being a rather self-aware and reflective anomaly is that you get to engage in the world in something of a tangential way and offer a take on life that is different – and hopefully helpful, positive and a way of changing the world just a little bit. I always say that I would love to leave the world in a better place when my time comes to leave it than it was when I came into it. My books – including this one – form a large part of that goal.

I wish you a good life and every success, my wonderful readers – and Sunflower the kitty sends you lots of virtual purrs.

Yennski

Notes

1. Neurokin is a term that refers to the people who share your neurotype: dyspraxia, ADHD, autism, neurotypical. Neurokinship enables pride, confidence.
2. Applied Behaviour Analysis (ABA) is a "therapy" for autism that is discredited by many and has been known to result in post-traumatic stress for some of those it was used on. Based in a rewards-and-punishments model, it seems more concerned about making children look somehow "less autistic" than in actually supporting their development. Behaviour training focuses on making kids stop stimming and often forces eye contact. We definitely do not condone ABA at Yennski's house!
3. "Controlled challenges" refers to putting in place incrementally more difficult activities to build confidence, competence, and resilience.

Assignments and discussion points

Consider: What are some of the communication differences between neurodivergent and neurotypical people?

Consider: What societal attitudes help – and hinder – inclusion for neurodivergent people?

Consider: What are some of the protective factors for inclusion and well-being?

Consider: What empowers neurodivergent people to engage in society?

Consider: What are the barriers to social and economic inclusion for neurodivergent people?

References

Amaze. (2023). Creating Change [Online] Available at: www.amaze.org.au/creating-change/research/employment/ [Accessed 1 April 2024].

Amaze. (2023). Autism and education in Australia. [Online] Available at: www.amaze.org.au/creating-change/research/community-attitudes-education/ [Accessed 20 April 2024].

American Psychiatric Association, DSM-5 Task Force. (2013). *Diagnostic and Statistical Manual of Mental Disorders: DSM-5™* (5th ed). American Psychiatric Publishing, Washington DC.

Aspect / Autism Spectrum Australia. (2023) About Autism [Online] Available at: www.autismspectrum.org.au/about-autism?gad_source=1&gclid=CjwKCAiA8sauBhB3EiwAruTRJnNp0LiuOjfmx5BSqnZR6un4-P0Zop4IRMCun8xTsaxhBrhYthXZBRoCAWoQAvD_BwE [Accessed 19 February 2024].

Aspect / Autism Spectrum Australia (2017). Sensory processing. [Online] Available at: www.aspect.org.au/uploads/documents/Fact%20Sheets/Factsheet_Sensory-processing_20170306.pdf [Accessed 4 April 2024].

Australian Bureau of Statistics (2023)[Online] Available at: https://www.abs.gov.au/ [accessed 5 March 2024]

Autistic Self Advocacy Network. (2024)What we believe [Online] Available at: autisticadvocacy.org/ [Accessed 19 February 2024].

Baron-Cohen, S. (1985). Does the Autistic Child Have "Theory of Mind"? *Cognition,* 21(1), pp. 37–46.

Broderick, A. A., and Ne'eman, A. (2008). Autism as Metaphor: Narrative and Counter-Narrative. *International Journal of Inclusive Education* , 12(5–6), pp. 459–476.

Centre for Intersectional Justice. (2023). What is intersectionality?[Online] Available at: www.intersectionaljustice.org/what-is-intersectionality [Accessed 14 March 2024].

Chloé Hayden website. (2023) *About Chloe* [Online] Available at: www.chloehayden.com.au/about-chloe [Accessed 22 January 2024].

Cooper, R. et al. (2021). "I'm Proud to Be a Little Bit Different": The Effects of Autistic Individuals' Perceptions of Autism and Autism Social Identity on Their Collective Self-Esteem, *Journal of Neurodevelopmental Disorders,* 51, pp. 704–714.

George, R. (2017). Sexual Orientation in Autism Spectrum Disorder. *Autism Research,* 11(1), pp. 133–141.

Gibbs, V., and Pellicano, E. (2023). "Maybe we just seem like easy targets": A Qualitative Analysis of Autistic Adults' Experiences of Interpersonal Violence. *Autism,* 27(7), pp. 2021–2034.

Glaves, K. J. et al. (2023) .Gender Diversity in Autistic Clients: An Ethical Perspective. *Frontiers in Psychiatry,* 14, p. 1244107.

Griffiths, A. et al. (2020). Developing Employment Environments Where Individuals with ASD Thrive: Using Machine Learning to Explore Employer Policies and Practices. *Brain Science* 10(9), p. 632.

Kupferstein H. (2018). Evidence of Increased PTSD Symptoms in Autistics Exposed to Applied Behavior Analysis. *Advances in Autism,* 4(1), pp. 19–29.

Martin, Jeffrey J., (2017) *Supercrip Identity - Handbook of Disability Sport and Exercise Psychology* Nova Publishers, New York

Masterman T and Purkis Y (2020) *The Awesome Autistic Go To Guide,* Jessica Kingsley Publishers, London

Merriam-Webster's Dictionary (2023). What are microaggressions? [Online] Available at: www.merriam-webster.com/dictionary/microaggression [Accessed 22 January 2024].

Milton, D., Gurbuz, E. and López, B. (2022). The "Double Empathy Problem": Ten Years on. *Autism*, 26(8), 1901–1903

National Autistic Society. (2024). Anxiety. [Online] Available at: www.autism.org.uk/advice-and-guidance/topics/mental-health/anxiety#:~:text=the%20NHS%20website.-,Why%20might%20autistic%20people%20experience%20anxiety%3F,a%20clinical%20diagnosis%20of%20anxiety [Accessed 14 April 2024].

People with Disability Australia. (2022). Social model of disability. [Online] Available at: https://pwd.org.au/resources/models-of-disability/ [Accessed 26 January 2024].

Purkis, Y and Cook, B (2023) *Planning Your Career Through Intense Interests*, Jessica Kingsley Publishers, London

Purkis, Y, (2006) *Finding a Different Kind of Normal*, Jessica Kingsley Publishers, London

Purkis, Y. (2024) [Blog] Yenn Purkis autism page. Available at: https://yennpurkis.home.blog/ [Accessed 24 May 2024].

Purkis, Y. (2018). [Blog] Yenn Purkis thoughts on all things autism and mental health. Available at: https://yennski.com/ [Accessed 24 May 2024].

Purkis, Y., and Goodall, E. (2017). *The Parents' Practical Guide to Resilience for Children Aged 2–10 on the Autism Spectrum*. Jessica Kingsley Publishers, London

Reframing Autism. (2023). I am an ally.[Online] Available at: https://reframingautism.org.au/service/i-am-an-ally/#:~:text=Being%20an%20ally%20goes%20further,faced%20and%20continue%20to%20face [Accessed 20 March 2024].

Reframing Autism. (2023). Understanding autism. [Online] Available at: https://reframingautism.org.au/about-autism/ [Accessed 20 March 2024].

Reframing Autism. (2023). Take the mask off: But what if I don't know how? [Online] Available at: https://reframingautism.org.au/takethemaskoff-but-what-if-i-dont-know-how/ [Accessed 3 March 2024].

Scheeren, A. (2021). The Importance of Home: Satisfaction with Accommodation, Neighbourhood, and Life in Adults with Autism. *Autism Research,* 15(3), pp. 519–530. Available at: https://doi.org/10.1002/aur.2653 [Accessed 3 March 2024].

Sequenza, A. (2018). Autism conversion therapy. [Online] Autism Women and Non-binary Network. Available at: https://awnnetwork.org/autistic-conversion-therapy/ [Accessed: 3 March 2024].

Silbermen, S. (2016). *Neurotribes.* Allen and Unwin. New York, USA

Simsion, G. (2015). *The Rosie Project: A Novel.* Test Publishing, Melbourne, Australia.

Specialisterne USA. (2022). Honesty is authenticity. [Online] Available at: https://us.specialisterne.com/honesty-is-authenticity/ [Accessed 22 January 2024].

Stonewall UK. (2023). Ace in the UK report. [Online] Available at: www.stonewall.org.uk/system/files/ace_in_the_uk_report_2023.pdf [Accessed 25 March 2024].

Strauss, J. (2013). *Autism as Culture*, Disability Studies Reader, pp. 462–474

Suarez, M. (2018). Sensory Processing in Children with Autism Spectrum Disorders and Impact on Functioning. *Paediatric Clinics of North America*, 59(1), pp. 203–214.

Summer Farrelly website. (2023). [Online] Available at: https://summerfarrelly.com.au/ [Accessed 22 January 2024]

Wang, P., and Spilane, A. (2009). Evidence-Based Social Skills Interventions for Children with Autism: A Meta-analysis. *Education and Training in Developmental Disabilities*, pp. 318–342.

Recommended further readings

The Autism and Neurodiversity Self-Advocacy Handbook, Barb Cook, Yenn Purkis, 2022, Jessica Kingsley Publishers

Finding a Different Kind of Normal, Yenn (Jeanette) Purkis, 2006, Jessica Kingsley Publishers

The Guide to Good Mental Health on the Autism Spectrum Yenn (Jeanette) Purkis, Emma Goodall, Jane Nugent, 2015, Jesscia Kinglsey Publishers

In Our Words, Yenn Purkis and Wayne Herbert, 2024, Lived Places Publishing

A Life Lived Well as an Autistic and Non-Binary Mental Health Advocate, Yenn Purkis, 2022, Lived Places Publishing

Neurotribes, Steve Silberman, 2016, Allen and Unwin,

Yenn Purkis' website: www.yennpurkis.com

Index

ableism. 5, 15, 19, 47, 80, 88, 110, 127

access to healthcare. 46

accommodation. 131–39

advocacy. 10, 18–20, 26–27, 41, 43, 47, 94; and allies. 57–60; reasons for the need of. 44–47; self-advocacy. 19–20, 47–49

aesthetic attraction. 92

alexithymia. 8–9

allies. 56–60

Alternative and Augmented Communication (AAC) device. 58

anxiety. 25, 76, 107, 115, 131, 135, 138; management of. 107–10; and perfectionism. 55, 56; and sensory processing issues. 97, 101, 105

applied behaviour analysis (ABA). 7, 62

asexuality. 87, 88, 91–93

Asperger's syndrome. 4

assistance animals. 117–19

autism. 22; challenges faced by autistic children. 39; conditions overlapping with. 97; de-medicalisation of challenges. 41; *DSM-5* diagnostic criteria for. 31–35; positive attributes of. 3; spectrum. 13, 15; therapies for. 23–24; training. 13, 46

autistic communication. 6, 22, 32, 61–65, 78

autistic community. 76–79

autistic culture. 5–10, 62–65, 78

autistic identity 3, 4–5

autistic pride. 13–20, 28; and disability funding. 37–40; Neurodiversity Pride Day. 25–27; parent's guide to. 20–25

Autistic Pride Day. 20

Autistic Self-Advocacy Network. 38, 76

autistic space. 77–79

bathrooms, gender neutral. 14

communication; and advocacy. 58–59; autistic. 6, 22, 61–65, 78; of sensory difficulties. 100–03; of sensory experience. 98

controlled challenges. 52, 55, 128

deep breathing. 109

diagnosis; *DSM-5* diagnostic criteria for autism. 31–35; of neurodivergent conditions. 35–37; psychiatric misdiagnosis. 13

disability; funding, and autistic pride. 37–40; and infantilism. 11; medical model of. 29, 30, 31, 35, 36–40, 42; social model of. 29–30, 35–40, 41, 42

discrimination. 6, 11, 21, 26, 47, 98, 110, 121, 126

distraction, for anxiety management. 109

double empathy problem. 65–66

DSM-5 diagnostic criteria for autism. 31–35

DXC Dandelion programme. 130

educational attainment of autistic people. 45–46

emotion blindness. *see* alexithymia

empathy. 8, 17, 44, 65–69

employment. 45, 121–22, 127; and disclosure/coming out. 125–27; and passionate interests. 122–23

exclusionary practices of autism organisations. 46

failure, successful. 53–56

friendships. 69–70, 73–76

funding, disability. 37–40

gender. *see also* sexuality; coming out. 15, 125–27; expression. 14

gender diversity. 46, 81–82; gender affirmation. 84–87; International Trans Day of Visibility. 82–83; and microaggressions. 13–14, 15, 16–17

gender-neutral bathrooms. 14

greysexuality. 89, *see also* asexuality

grief. 67

honesty of autistic people. 8, 32, 61

housing. 131–39

I CAN Network. 45

identity. 28, *see also* gender; autistic. 3, 4–5; and autistic pride. 18, 26, 27; and diagnosis of neurodivergent conditions. 36–37; and imposter syndrome. 115; and language. 12; and masking. 72; and self-advocacy. 20

imposter syndrome. 113–16

incels. 93

inclusion. 9, 10, 17, 19, 38, 43, 46, 56, 58, 64, 70, 76, 82, 94, 113, 119, 123

incompetence, assumptions of. 12, 115

infantilism. 11–12, 87

inspiration porn. 40

International Trans Day of Visibility. 82–83

interoception. 95, 104–05

intersectionality. 11, 17, 116; and allies. 56; and imposter syndrome. 114–15

language. 9, 12, *see also* communication

legacy thinking. 46

manipulation, and autistic people. 8, 32

masking. 69–73, 133

media. 46–47

medical model of disability. 29, 30, 31; and diagnosis. 35, 36–37; and disability funding. 37–40

medications for anxiety. 108

mental health; anxiety management. 107–10; imposter syndrome. 113–16; pets and assistance animals. 117–19; services. 110–13

microaggressions. 10–14, 15, 16–17

mindfulness. 109

misgendering. 13–14, 17

neurodiversity. 6, 9, 13, 30–31, 36, 38, 63, 76

Neurodiversity Pride Day. 19, 25–27

neurokinship. 6

non-verbal cues. 8

object permanence. 65, 67

parents. 26; and advocacy. 57; Parent's Guide to Autistic Pride, A (Purkis). 20–25

perfectionism. 55, 56

pets. 117–19

practical empathy. 67–68

pride. *see* autistic pride

proprioception. 96

psychiatric misdiagnosis. 13

psychosis. 25, 108, 110, 111, 135, 138

relationships. 69–70; approach to. 32; ex-friends. 73–76; intimate. 88–91, 92–93; and masking. 69–73

resilience. 21, 49; importance of. 50–53; and successful failure. 53–56

role models. 23, 83

romantic attraction. 90–91

Safer Girls Safer Women. 87

schizophrenia. 27, 36, 48, 128, 133, 134, 136

self-advocacy. 19–20

self-confidence. 21, 34, 51, 55, 115–16, 128

self-doubt. 113–16

self-esteem. 21, 23, 51, 72, 123

sensory accessibility. 96, 99–100

sensory processing disorder (SPD). 95, 104

sensory processing issues. 41; addressing. 95–96; communication of sensory difficulties. 100–03; impact of. 97–99, 104; and interpretation of reality. 104; invalidation/dismissal of. 98, 105; and sex. 89

sensory room. 112

sexuality. 46, 82, 87–88, 90–91, *see also* gender; and intimate relationships. 88–91

social media. 85; and autistic community. 76; and coming out. 15

social model of disability. 29–30, 41; and diagnosis. 35–37; and disability funding. 37–40

Specialisterne. 130

stimming. 23, 24

subterfuge, and autistic people. 8

successful failure. 53–56

supercrip. 40

theory of mind. 65

thoughts, and anxiety management. 108

Trans Day of Visibility. 82–83

Transgender Day of Remembrance. 82

woke culture. 10

workplace. 121, 126; challenges. 123; managers in. 123, 124; sensory accessibility in. 96, 99–100

World Autism Awareness Day. 19

Yellow Ladybugs. 45

www.ingramcontent.com/pod-product-compliance
Lightning Source LLC
Chambersburg PA
CBHW060836190426
43197CB00040B/2655